on-the-edge games

for Youth Ministry

by Karl Rohnke

Group
Loveland, Colorado

On-the-Edge Games for Youth Ministry

Copyright © 1998 Karl Rohnke

Credits

Co-author: Cindy Hansen
Editor: Amy Simpson
Chief Creative Officer: Joani Schultz
Copy Editor: Candace McMahan
Art Director: Ray Tollison
Cover Art Director: Jeff A. Storm
Cover Designer: Becky Hawley
Computer Graphic Artist: Lighthouse Communications Group
Cover Photographer: Jafe Parsons
Illustrator: Simon Lovell
Production Manager: Gingar Kunkel

Library of Congress Cataloging-in-Publication Data
Rohnke, Karl.
    On-the-edge games for youth ministry / by Karl Rohnke.
       p. cm.
    Includes indexes.
    ISBN 0-7644-2058-5
    1. Church group work with teenagers. 2. Games in Christian education. I. Title.
    BV4447.R65 1998
    268'.433—dc21   98-15310
                                                  CIP

10 9 8 7 6 5 4 3 2 1   07 06 05 04 03 02 01 00 99 98

Printed in the United States of America.

Contents

Introduction

Using These Games

The games in this book and of this genre are meant to be shared, adapted, changed, and fully enjoyed. Although the text in this book is copyrighted, the ideas are absolutely up for grabs. A good idea doesn't care who has it, and thank goodness for that. So play them as indicated, then change the play to fit your situation and group. Change the names, too, if that fits your need. It's a great empowerment ploy to allow a group of players to name a game that's brand-new to them. Take a look at these other game-teaching suggestions:

- Establish a comfortable relationship with the players right away. Talk, share, compare, smile, and be at ease.
- Extend an obvious, well-heard, and open welcome to all new (late) players.
- Establish yourself as a player as well as the leader right from the start. Personalize the game with your person.
- Begin with games that include movement and have few, easily explained rules.
- Let the players stretch their bodies and their feelings slowly at first: no running, no competition, no contact—yet.
- Explain the game's structure and rules as clearly and simply as possible, and do it in a way that encourages participation, playfulness, fantasy, and fun. You are the game master.
- Combine description with demonstration, facial gymnastics, and no-holds histrionics. Don't lecture!
- After a period of play, ask for questions about the game. If a particular question suggests an interesting variation, use it as an opportunity to empower the players, allowing the group to take charge of the game.
- Always offer people choices. A coerced player is no longer a player
- Encourage the group, through participation, to begin to understand the value of shared stupidity. Demonstrate the games with appropriately outrageous or foolish words and actions, then encourage your players to join you.

Tips for Teaching Games

- Before a physically active game, point out areas that require special safety procedures. (For example, big people watch out for little people.)
- When explaining rules, set a tone indicating that rules should be followed only as long as the group wants to follow them. Be open to changing rules.
- Know the games well enough to help change them.
- Break the mold of everyday language. Every now and then, say something that gets the players to think. Instead of saying, "Form a circle," say, "Line up in a circle." Instead of saying, "Form pairs," say, "Form dyads." Instead of "fifty," say, "half a hundred."
- You'll know when a game is too long—attention wanes. Move on.

Use these games as pure recreation, or present them as a means for players to learn more about teamwork and about themselves. Brief post-game discussions can lead to profound differences in future group functioning and sometimes in life itself. Consider using the Learning Options throughout the book. They'll help you extend a game into a discussion on fleeing from temptation, teamwork, the body of Christ, gossip, the future, or putting faith into action—to name just a few. You can also lead your own discussion because many of the games naturally lead into questions of trust, peer pressure, efficiency and productivity, competition, fear (forget everything and run), and commitment.

But when all's said and read, play for the joy of total sentient involvement in something that's fun to do. It's so-o-o-o simple...

About the Authors

Karl Rohnke

As a sixty-year-old only child, I consider myself to be a highly qualified games person. Considering my six decades of fooling around, if you count back you'll find that I spent most of my official childhood in the early 1940s (i.e., pre-television). What a stupendous time for imagination and creativity! I consider myself extremely lucky to have spent at least ten years unencumbered by the brain-numbing effects of the tube.

I spent a number of those early years in Staten Island, New York, not exactly what I'd call a vacation spot. But my memories of role-playing, making our own action toys, and not being programmed by adults are the best. In some ways I wish I could have provided less for my own children.

After spending more years being a kid than most, I more or less earned a degree in biology from Washington and Lee University. Actually, it could have been a degree in anything because I was interested in everything.

After a couple of years in the Army, I tried a stint in the merchant marine, tried my hand as a medical technologist in a geriatric living/dying community, and finally worked as an outdoor-education-trail teacher for the Long Beach Unified School District in California (basically leading nature hikes and seizing the teachable moment to pass along information about bio-cycles and ecology—the biology degree paid off!).

After about five years of trail-teaching, night hikes, and leading campfire activities, I was ready for a dramatic change. With alacrity, I immersed myself in the programmed discomforts of the Outward Bound curriculum and set myself above the students by not only accepting the various challenges but reveling in them. I did not facilitate; I impelled—all because of my personal mastery of the moment and a humongous helping of ego. But four years of constant ego maintenance and living in the woods could wear anyone down, and my "pads" were wearing thin.

An educational initiative in Massachusetts called Project Adventure was looking for someone who could build a ropes course and implement an adventure curriculum in a public school setting. I had built two ropes courses at that point (twice as many as most people), and adventure was my middle name.

I got the job and genuinely enjoyed building Project Adventure's first ropes course during the summer months of 1971. When school started in September, my well-manicured adventure persona took a big hit; the high school students were not responding to my practiced do-it-because-I-know-more-than-you "teaching" style. Also, curriculum that had been functional during a twenty-six-day residential "survival" experience was shunned by physical education students who knew that their entire commitment to me would be no more than thirty minutes, three times a week. I thought my days at Project Adventure were limited, and I didn't really care because I was convinced that my wilderness "...and not to yield" approach was valid and could be applied elsewhere.

My wife was less cavalier about leaving. She had borne the brunt of the last move and was not about to move again. I soon recollected a quote I'd once heard, paraphrased here: "If you're interested in young people doing what you want them to do, find out what they want, then tell them to do it." Recognizing that no one was telling or even suggesting to us (PA staff) what to do, I asked the students what they wanted to do, then suggested a few atypical games and activities that I used to play as a kid. The combination of the students knowing that someone cared enough to ask and my suggestion of physical happenings that had nothing to do with push-ups, pull-ups, or sit-ups was key.

The program caught fire, and I was on the way to a fun-based career. The big change for me was recognizing that the simple affording of choice could achieve more toward growth of self-awareness and self-image than what used to require large doses of performance pressure. With the pressure off both the student and the teacher, the opportunity for growth was palpably different. I discovered a remarkably sentient aspect to teaching that I had missed. Actually, it had been masked and blunted by my years of ego satisfaction and my adherence to a one-minded, often glandular approach.

As adult years approached (somewhere around forty), I kept anticipating what everyone was predicting: "Karl, one of these days you're going to have to grow up." Well, other than getting married, having four children, holding down a job, leading workshops, losing hair, writing books...I still consider myself fairly childlike, and that's a win-win situation. A win for me because I think differently from most adults I know, and a win for you because of what appears in books like this one.

Cindy Hansen

As a forty-one-year-old Karl Rohnke fan, I consider myself highly qualified to work with him on this fun game book. Take a look at my background and the Karl Rohnke connections.

In 1978, I received my bachelor of arts degree in recreation from Bethany College in Lindsborg, Kansas. After that, I worked as a recreation specialist in the parks and recreation department in Loveland, Colorado. I used games by Karl in my programs with youth and adults of all ages.

At that time, I also was a youth sponsor at my church. Karl's games worked great at youth group meetings, retreats, and camps. Kids loved them. Often, after we played a game or two, the discussion would naturally lead into topics such as communication and teamwork. I also used the games to connect to a Bible study point.

After a few years, I went back to school and received my master of arts degree in education. I did my student teaching in England, and I took my Karl Rohnke bag of tricks along. Guess what? Regardless of age, country, or situation, people love the games...and the games naturally lead into discussions on a variety of topics.

Through the years, I've gained a husband, who's a pastor, and three boys, who are an energetic delight. I also went to work for an interdenominational Christian publishing company, Group Publishing.

My experience and education have combined to qualify me for my current position as program coordinator for camps and conferences at Group. I love my job. What better way to use the games, discussions, and lead-ins to Bible studies?

Outside of work, I currently teach middle school Sunday school at our church. One of my fellow teachers, Mike Krantz, works for a parks and recreation department. He brought in a whole pile of Karl Rohnke game books to help with our Sunday school planning. We thought, "If we use Karl Rohnke games to lead into our Bible study topics, why shouldn't other people do the same?"

Meanwhile, back at the ranch (Group Publishing, that is), other people had heard of Karl Rohnke's games, and the wheels were set in motion.

And thus...the book *On-the-Edge Games for Youth Ministry*. After each game, we've included a Learning Option to guide you with your youth group in discussion and Bible study.

Have a blast with your own Karl connection, and God bless you in your ministry with kids.

— Cindy

Crowdbreakers

Bow Knots

Activity Level: low

Activity Area: anywhere

Supplies: kids' shoes with shoelaces

game tip

Have shoestring-shod kids share a shoe with loafer- or Velcro-shod kids.

The Game: Ask participants to untie and retie their shoes and note the different finger manipulations used to accomplish the common bow knot. Note the different tying techniques—it's amazing.

The highly complex knot arrangement that holds your shoes onto your feet is usually taught by family and is as sure an indication of your lineage as any other cultural touchstone.

Are the laces thrown across one another at the start? Definitely Germanic. Or are the twin strands folded and placed just so? This purposeful start indicates French lineage. If the laces are turned concurrently into two equal loops and tied directly together (the so-called Bunny Ears technique), you might rightly suspect an Italian or Scandinavian background. Think so? Academicians take note—here's a thesis topic I'm sure no one has tackled.

Once participants have practiced untying and retying their shoes, get ready for a speed contest by designating a common starting position:

- laces draped toward the floor on each side of the shoe
- one lace in each hand

Say: **When I give a signal, see who can tie your shoes the fastest. Ready? Tie!**

Watch finger dexterity at work.

Variation: Have participants teach their shoe-tying techniques to one another then race again using a new tying technique.

Learning Option: I'm Unique

Themes: God's love, personality, uniqueness

One at a time, have kids show their personal preferences for shoe tying. Afterward, have them say something unique about themselves—something people wouldn't know by looking at them. For example, "I like to eat M&M's with popcorn when I watch movies" or "I traveled to Africa when I was four years old."

After everyone has shared, have students take turns reading a verse in Psalm 139 until they've read the entire psalm. Give a prayer of thanks to God, who made each one of us unique in amazing and wonderful ways.

Foot-to-Foot Pass

Activity Level: high

Activity Area: large classroom, gymnasium, or outside

Supplies: an inflated beach ball

The Game: Excuse me for being so simplistic, but the following game is fun. Have players take off their shoes and sit in a circle. Ask all participants to say their names a couple of times. Instruct them to pass an inflated beach ball around the circle, using only their feet or ankles. Each time a player passes the ball, that person should say the name of the person he or she is passing it to. If all the players already know each other's names, have them say something else, such as their own favorite color or their own favorite hobby.

If kids drop the ball, have them use their hands to pick it up and continue the foot-to-foot manipulations. If you're attempting this game on a polished gym floor, have players rotate on their posteriors to make the pass from person to person. It's an impressive motion and fun to do.

After you've completed a couple of semisuccessful rounds, you're ready for action. Form two or three equal-numbered teams, and have them collect at one end of the playing area—a basketball court, a field house, a polo field, a parking lot, or a par-five golf hole—and get set for some serious foot-to-foot competition.

Have each team sit in a line. The object is to pass the ball from one end of the playing field to the other, using only the feet of the players on each team—exactly like the warm-up at the beginning of this activity. Players say the names of the people they're passing the ball to, then they pass the ball. They extend the line by peeling off from the initial position, running to the end of the line, sitting there, and preparing to pass the ball when it comes to them again (you know, the old infinite-line trick). First ball to the end of the expanse wins.

game tip

Be sure to adjust the game and the playing area to the size of your group as necessary. If you have a small group, don't have them form teams; have everyone play together. And you may want to play in a smaller area so the game doesn't last too long and players don't lose interest.

Of course the winners gain great stature in their own eyes and occasionally in the estimation of easily impressed observers. This elevated status lasts about thirty seconds or so, or until the next round begins. For each new round, mix the lineup so kids learn more new names or new information about more new people.

Learning Option: The Messenger's Feet

Themes: God's love, sharing faith

Gather at the end of the playing area, and let players rest their feet. Read Mark 6:6-13, the passage describing Jesus' sending his disciples out to teach and spread the good news. Ask:

● **What was it like to play this game?**

● **How was it like spreading the good news of God's love to others? How was it different?**

Reread Mark 6:11: "And if any place will not welcome you or listen to you, shake the dust off your feet when you leave, as a testimony against them." Ask:

● **When is it difficult to share your faith?**

● **Why is it hard to handle laughter or ridicule or people not taking you seriously?**

● **What did Jesus mean when he told his disciples to "shake the dust off [their] feet" when people wouldn't listen to them?**

● **How can you "shake the dust off your feet" when someone doesn't listen to you when you share your faith?**

Close in prayer, asking for God's strength to spread the good news and for help to "shake the dust off [our] feet" when people don't listen. Offer thanks for Jesus' example of ministry and love.

How Ya Doin'?

Activity Level: low

Activity Area: large classroom, gymnasium, or outside

Supplies: one blindfold for each person

The Game: Have kids stand shoulder-to-shoulder in a circle. Give each person a blindfold to put on. When everyone is blindfolded, have the players count off and remember their numbers. (If you have more than fifteen players, have them form two groups.)

When the players are circled up, numbered, and waiting, have them ask the people to their immediate right and left this question: "How ya doin'?" Each person asked will answer: "Jus' fine, thanks!" Continue this verbal flood until all players hear the repetitive Q and A at least three times.

Say: **What you're saying and hearing is essential toward the solution of the problem I'm about to present. When I give a signal, you'll mill around the room blindfolded. Make a body bumper by placing your hands up, palms forward. This will protect you in the milling process. Say "Milling, milling, milling," while you move to let each other know you're not alone in this exercise. Besides, it sounds funny.**

Here's the problem: After you've milled around for one minute, you have to return to your initial numbered position, standing shoulder-to-shoulder in a circle. You can talk during this reorganization, but the only thing you can say is "How ya doin'?" and "Jus' fine, thanks!" reiterated as many times as you'd like. Ready? Start milling.

After one minute of milling, say: **Line up in a circle.** (Line up in a circle? Are you kidding? No, really. You can do that.) You and they may be surprised at the sequential accuracy of the final circle. I'm not surprised. I've done this before.

Learning Option: Listening for God's Voice

Themes: God's voice, listening to God

Have kids form two groups. Assign each group one of these Scriptures to read:

- John 10:27-28
- 1 Kings 19:11-13

Have groups discuss the following question and be ready to report their answers to the large group: "What does your passage say about listening for God's voice?"

After a few moments, get reports from the two groups. They might say something like "Jesus is the shepherd; we are the sheep. The sheep listen for and know the shepherd's voice." Or "Sometimes we look for God's voice in loud noises like earthquakes, wind, and fire. But sometimes God's voice is still and quiet."

Play the game again, using the same rules, only this time use this question and answer: "Who ya gonna listen to?" "God's voice."

I Like It

Activity Level: low

Activity Area: classroom

Supplies: newsprint, markers, and masking tape

The Game: Use this game as a means of getting kids to know one another. Ask your group to brainstorm ten characteristics they'd like to discover about one another. Record these characteristics on a piece of newsprint, writing large enough to allow everyone to see. These characteristics might include such things as favorite pizza topping, best thing to do on a Saturday afternoon, best thing to do on summer vacation, best book read in the last year, top movie of the year, favorite thing to hate, pet pedagogic peeve, and top recreational pursuit.

Then, asking for a show of majority (elevated hands, voice volume, basic intimidation), pick the top three characteristics.

Give each player a marker and a sheet of newsprint. Have players write their answers to the top three characteristics. Provide about two or three minutes for this on-the-fly soul-searching.

As you see people finishing, use masking tape to attach their papers "billboard-style" to their backs. Then have kids form groups of four, and have each person describe his or her characteristics as the rest of the foursome looks at the "billboard." When everyone has completed the show and tell, have everyone in each foursome try to remember the others' characteristics without looking at the billboards.

Once groups of four know each other well, increase the size of groups until the whole class knows each person's interesting characteristics and can recall them without looking at the billboards. Think of this activity as the ultimate getting-to-know-you game.

Learning Option: One of a Kind

Themes: affirmation, body of Christ, personality, uniqueness

Have kids take off their billboards and write their names on them. Then have kids sit in a circle and pass the billboards to the right. Have kids write one admirable thing about the person whose billboard is in front of them. Have kids keep passing and writing until everyone has signed all the billboards. After kids have retrieved their own billboards, give them a moment to read the affirmations.

Have kids put their billboards back on and link arms. Read aloud: "Now you are the body of Christ, and each one of you is a part of it" (1 Corinthians 12:27). Close in prayer, thanking God for each person's unique gifts as a part of the body of Christ.

Loafers Rule

Activity Level: medium

Activity Area: classroom or gymnasium

Supplies: kids' shoes

The Game: I don't know what it is that people like about taking off their shoes and using them as game equipment, but they do like it. So here's a game that involves doing just that.

Have players sit in a circle, remove both shoes, and place them in a center pile. (Hold the olfactory comments, please.) Have players close their eyes while you mix the shoes.

Say: **Open your eyes. In a moment, find one of your shoes and one that belongs to someone else. This requires that you remember what your shoes look like—concentrate.** (Don't play this game blindfolded, or kids will miss dinner and perhaps their next birthday.)

Say: **Put your shoe on your foot, then find that special someone who belongs to the second shoe—your Cinderella, so to speak—gender notwithstanding. Share names and something personal, such as shoe size. Keep it short because there's lots of shoe sharing going on. Share facts, not personal biographies.**

After shoe- and fact-sharing are finished, ask players to sit in a circle again. Have the partners introduce each other and succinctly relate what they've been told by each other.

If simply finding a shoeless foot seems too tame, require that after a player has identified his or her "sole mate," the pair must down a pint of Ben & Jerry's Chunky Monkey ice cream in less than fifteen minutes, then run a mile with each other's shoes on. Wild? Ya gotta love it! Am I kidding? Does a chicken have lips?

Learning Option: Seeking Good

Themes: body of Christ, servanthood, unselfishness

Play the game again. Have participants pile their shoes in the center of the room and close their eyes while you mix them. Then have kids open their eyes and listen while you read 1 Corinthians 10:24: "Nobody should seek his own good, but the good of others."

Say: **Play the game again, finding one of your shoes and one of someone else's. When you search and find your Cinderella, each of you share your name and what you think that verse means to you today. Ready? Seek and find.**

Gather shod participants in a circle, and encourage them to discuss their insights. Close with prayer, asking God to help us keep our eyes off ourselves and to be on the lookout for ways to help others.

Mass Movement

Activity Level: medium

Activity Area: large classroom, gymnasium, or outside

Supplies: a one-inch-wide roll of masking tape for every six to eight players

The Game: Gather players at one end of the game area. Form even-numbered teams of six to eight kids. Ask players in each team to line up shoulder-to-shoulder, facing alternately in opposite directions (see illustration below).

Give a full roll of one-inch masking tape to a person at the end of each line (either end, doesn't matter). Ask that person to stick the tape end firmly to his or her body at about waist level, wrap the tape around a full turn, and pass the roll to the next person in line, who will repeat the full-turn process and pass it on, and so forth down the line. Have players keep wrapping themselves in this manner until the tape is used up.

Then say to the sticky queues: **Your team's goal is to walk across the playing area and back, keeping your line intact. If someone tears off and separates from the line, do a quick patch job and continue on.**

Don't bother with penalties for "tearing away." Taping each other and attempting to move as a team is more important than quality of performance.

If you inadvertently substitute a roll of fiberglass tape for this team experience, the group bonding might be a bit more permanent than you bargained for. But if there's some duct tape around...

Learning Option: Looking Out for Each Other

Themes: body of Christ, friendship, servanthood, working together

Have kids stay bunched together. Give each bunch a Bible, and have kids work together to find and read Ecclesiastes 4:9-12. Ask:

- **What was it like to work together to do this task?**
- **How did you need one other to get the job done?**
- **How do we need others in our lives?**
- **What keeps us from asking others for help?**

Help kids get untaped, then gather the used tape in a ball. Pass the sticky ball from person to person, and have each one mention one way he or she will help someone over the next week. Close with a group hug, thanking God for placing everyone together as a group.

Thumbs Up

Activity Level: low

Activity Area: anywhere

Supplies: one photocopy of the "Print Someone Who…" handout (p. 23) and an ink pad for each person

game tip

Instead of giving each person an ink pad, you can place several ink pads at various places around the room, within easy reach of the thumb-print collectors. Or you could give each person a water-based marker to use as "ink."

The Game: This getting-to-know-you game identifies everyone as a thumb-print collector. The collection of smudgy prints serves as proof that kids have discovered valuable information about one another.

Give each player a copy of the handout and an ink pad.

Say: **You have five minutes to collect as many different thumb prints as you can on your sheet. You can get more than one person's thumb print for each item on your handout. You can use each person's thumb print only once. Start collecting.**

Variation: Have players collect big-toe prints rather than thumb prints.

Learning Option: Uniquely Yours

Themes: love, personality, uniqueness

Gather the thumb-print collections, and point out that no two prints are alike. Read Psalm 139 aloud, then discuss the good news that God cares so much about each person that he made us each unique.

game tip

The thumb prints are much easier and neater to obtain if each person holds a clipboard or a hardback book underneath the handout.

Have kids use their one-of-a-kind thumbs and fingers to give each other quick back rubs. Have them stand in a circle and face in one direction, giving the shoulders in front of them a one-minute rubdown. Then have them turn and face the opposite direction and give another pair of shoulders a one-minute rubdown.

Close by thanking God for the individuals in your group.

Print Someone Who...

...was born the same month as you.

...is wearing a red or green shirt.

...has a driver's license.

...is wearing braces.

...is wearing wrist or ankle jewelry.

...is two years younger than you.

...is wearing a "tucked-in" shirt.

...is wearing shoes with letters on the bottom.

...is wearing tie shoes. Untie one shoe and tie it back.

...has less hair than you.

...can sing. Have that person sing one verse of a well-known song and receive some applause.

Toss Up

Activity Level: high

Activity Area: gymnasium or outside

Supplies: one Nerf or fleece ball for each player

The Game: Ask the players to stand in a loose group so they can move about without bumping into one another. Give each player a Nerf or fleece ball (or any other ball that won't hurt if it bounces off someone's head).

This crowdbreaker is a great one for helping a group of students who barely know one another to learn one another's names.

The challenge starts by having one player toss a ball about ten feet into the air. Any player can make the first toss; it doesn't matter. When the person tosses the ball, he or she must say the name of another person in the group. Then that person must catch the ball.

If the ball is caught, two balls are then tossed simultaneously. Any two players can make the toss. Again, when the balls are tossed, each tossing player must call out the name of someone else in the group. Those two people must then catch the balls. At that point, three balls are tossed simultaneously and so on.

This systematic throw-and-catch challenge continues until one of the balls is dropped. At that point, the group begins again with one ball.

> **game tip**
>
> The challenge is best maintained if you tell everyone when to throw; otherwise, the group begins to delay the tosses to make catching easier. Also, be strict about the throws reaching at least ten feet in the air.

Learning Opti$_o$n: Working Together

Themes: body of Christ, communication, cooperation, teamwork, working together

Achieving multiple throws and catches (without a drop) requires communication (talking and listening) and cooperation (hold the ego) within the group. So after playing for a while, gather everyone and discuss these questions:

● **How successful has our tossing and catching been so far?**

● **How could we better work together to increase the number of successful attempts?**

Play another game of Toss Up, and see if the players can raise the number of successful tosses and catches. Then gather the group again, and discuss these questions:

● **How did our communication and cooperation affect our success in this game?**

● **What made the difference in the game this time?**

● **How is this like working together as Christians? How is it different?**

● **What do you need from others to help you in your life as a Christian?**

Read Ephesians 4:25–5:7, a passage in which Paul gives the Ephesians guidelines for living as the body of Christ. Then ask:

● **What specific things does Paul mention in this passage that we can do to help our fellow Christians?**

● **What are some specific ways we can provide these things for each other?**

Close with a silent prayer, encouraging each person to give thanks for the person to the right. Then play the game again, encouraging players to work together to attain a higher goal.

Warped Speed

Activity Level: low

Activity Area: classroom

Supplies: a stopwatch or a watch with a second hand on it

The Game: Here's all you need to do to achieve warped speed. Have kids form groups of no more than ten, and have each group line up in a circle. Starting with one person in each circle, see how fast kids in the group can say their first names in sequence all the way around the circle and back to the starting person.

Use a stopwatch to time each attempt. If you have more than one group, find a timer for each group. There's no real standard or point at which you know you've reached warped speed. You can tell, though, because at warped speed, everyone is cheering and really getting into the game. This is group competition at its best, with each group competing avidly against its own best effort.

Did kids learn any names as a result of playing this game? If so, that's an added benefit. The real benefits of the game are cooperation, communication, and fun.

> **game tip**
>
> Be animated as you present the challenge. The more cheerleading from the facilitator, the more enthusiasm from the players.

Variation 1: Send the name sequence in the opposite direction.

Variation 2: Send names in both directions at the same time.

> **game tip**
>
> If the chosen movements require wild swinging of the arms or legs, move the players a safe but still cozy distance apart.

Variation 3: Ask players to say the number of syllables in their names instead of saying their names. For example, instead of saying my name, "Karl," I'd say "one."

Variation 4: Say the number of syllables in your name, at the same time demonstrating a distinct body movement for each syllable; for example, one overhead clap, two foot stomps, or three wild twists.

This series of histrionic gesticulations establishes the basis for another one-time-only world-record attempt.

Variation 5: Have players say their names and demonstrate actions for each syllable. As each person does this, the other players must repeat his or her name and actions—adding each person's name and actions to the previous ones, until the entire circle of players' names and actions are learned.

_L_earning Opti_o_n: All in a Name

Themes: God's love, names

Invite kids to sit in a circle and share stories about their names: how they were named, people they were named after, whether or not they like their names, other names they wish were theirs—anything about their names.

Read Isaiah 43:1: "But now, this is what the Lord says—he who created you, O Jacob, he who formed you, O Israel: 'Fear not, for I have redeemed you; I have summoned you by name; you are mine.' "

Pray: **God, thank you for saving us. We thank you that each one of us is yours.** Have each person say his or her name, then say: **Amen.**

Wiggle-Waggle

Activity Level: low

Activity Area: classroom

Supplies: none

The Game: I'm not even going to try to put this well-known children's activity into words. Check out the illustrations below; they might bring back memories.

It's just a matter of rotating your hands in the proper direction. Put your hands in front of your face, palm to palm, then cross your middle fingers. If your right middle finger is closer to you, rotate your right palm away from you. If your left middle finger is closer to you, rotate your left palm away from you.

After you rotate, your middle fingers should be back to back, and your thumbs should match up with your pinkie fingers. Your hands should be parallel to the ground, and one middle finger should be pointing up in the air while the other is pointing down. Now wiggle and waggle your middle fingers. (I just said I wasn't going to try to write how to do this and…well, take it as a bonus, and don't listen to me next time.)

Present this wiggle-waggle manipulation, and ask players to duplicate the maneuver. Once everyone has mastered the manipulation or achieved some level of individual success, have players choose partners. Have partners give each other high fives, share first names, then do the Wiggle-Waggle with each other. To do this, partners must stand face-to-face, palm-to-palm, and rotate to the wiggle-waggle position.

Anticipate considerable laughter with much wiggle and sometimes no waggle. Let pairs work together for a while until some wiggle-waggle success is achieved. Then have partners use both hands at the same time to wiggle-waggle.

Next, have players form a circle with their hands at their sides in the classic gunfighter position. (If you don't know what that is, make something up.) When you say "Draw!" have kids do the Wiggle-Waggle thing with the people on their right and left simultaneously. After fifteen seconds say "stop." If anyone is still digitally fumbling around, the entire group is forfeit. Try group Wiggle-Waggle three times.

At the end of three attempts, ask the players if they'd evaluate their efforts as a success or failure. Wait for the responses. I think you'll be surprised and pleased at the depth of their perception. If achieving simultaneous wiggle-waggle was the goal, then the group may not have succeeded. If communicating, cooperating, trusting one another, and having outrageous fun were the goal, then success was achieved. It's worth talking about, and Wiggle-Waggle is worth doing.

Learning Option: Keep On Trying

Themes: failure, forgiveness, mistakes, sin, struggles

After many attempts, failures, and successes at Wiggle-Waggle, gather kids in a circle. Read Romans 7:14-25. Ask:

● **What struggle does Paul describe in this passage?**

● **What does verse 21 mean: "So I find this law at work: When I want to do good, evil is right there with me"?**

● **Why do we sometimes fail to do the right thing in life?**

● **When we make mistakes, how can we keep trying to do what's right?**

Offer a prayer, giving kids an opportunity to silently ask forgiveness for wrong things they've done. Offer thanks to God for his forgiveness and the strength he gives us to do what's right.

Say: **Even though we sometimes fail, God never fails us.** Close by reading 1 Chronicles 28:20: " **'Be strong and courageous, and do the work. Do not be afraid or discouraged, for the Lord God, my God, is with you. He will not fail you or forsake you...'** "

Trust Builders

D_o It!

Activity Level: high

Activity Area: gymnasium or outside

Supplies: none

The Game: Need a low-risk, minimum-skill, team- and trust-oriented, action-packed game? Here 'tis.

Form four equal-numbered groups. Nope...don't do that. Try the following instead. Ask each player to choose a number from one to four, but not to indicate in any way what that number is.

Say: **To discover the number you unknowingly share with other folks, mingle and shake hands. Purposefully pump your hand up and down as many times as will match the number you chose. If your number is two and someone tries to shake your hand three times, excuse yourself politely and continue your search for meaning, truth, and somebody who shares your number. When you find a hand moving up and down concurrently with yours, and if that hand stops at the appropriate number, keep that well-numbered person with you, and operating as a harmonic dyad, find another free spirit vibrating on your joint frequency. Continue linking numerically until you have established your affiliation with a one, two, three, or four group.**

Here comes your role: Stand in the middle of the playing area and hold out both arms parallel to the ground. Ask the four groups to orient themselves around you, standing in columns beginning at your front, back, and both sides (see illustration on page 32).

game tip

If you're lucky, each group will contain approximately the same number of people congratulating one another on their choice. I've been pursuing this exercise for the past twenty years and have never had the groups come out equally, so concentrate on gaining the satisfaction that comes from initiating something that's FUNN (Functional Understanding's Not Necessary) but not functional. Ask a few uncommitted players to change groups to equal things up. Most folks don't care what group they're in as long as fun is the focus.

Whatever position each group chooses becomes specific to that group. For example, each time you change position the groups must realign themselves in columns beginning at your front, back, or sides according to their initial positions.

Say: **I'm going to change position, but your group can't move until you hear me shout, "Do it!" At that signal, run to your new location. Remember, you are a trusting, "in-this-together" team. When your entire group forms a column, shout together, "All for one and one for all; we're together and having a ball." Shout the ditty as loudly and proudly as you can.**

The first group to gain its position and simultaneously belt out the all-for-one ditty is designated the winner of that round and, in all fairness, is roundly applauded by the other three teams.

Here are a few more rules:

● If a team moves before it hears "Do it," it forfeits that round.

● A team can't begin yelling the ditty until all of its members are at the proper location and are in line. Beginning the ditty before the line is established forfeits the round for that team.

Variation 1: Experience a more raucous version of the game by allowing teams to try to keep one another from reaching their destinations. This, of course, keeps the holders from reaching their destinations also, but there's certainly fun to be had in the attempt. Know your teams before you present this variation. If the group's trust and/or cooperative level is questionable, proceed to the next variation.

Variation 2: Slow down the teams as they run from location to location by assigning a Hula Hoop to each team and requiring each member to bodily pass through the hoop before the team can begin shouting the ditty. The diameter of the hoop has a lot to do with the increased difficulty. Be kind.

Learning Option: Doers of the Word

Themes: faith in action, good deeds, hypocrisy, integrity, servanthood, showing faith

Gather all groups in a circle and ask:

● **Are you a "doer" or a "thinker"? Are you more likely to act without thinking or think without acting?** Have kids give examples.

Read James 2:15-17: "Suppose a brother or sister is without clothes and daily food. If one of you says to him, 'Go, I wish you well; keep warm and well fed,' but does nothing about his physical needs, what good is it? In the same way, faith by itself, if it is not accompanied by action, is dead." Ask:

● **What does "faith by itself...is dead" mean?**

● **In what ways can we be "doers" of our faith?**

Brainstorm ways to be doers of the faith, perhaps by reaching out to needy people. You might suggest that the group collect food for a food pantry, gather clothes for an outreach center, or serve the community in some other way. As a group, choose one idea and schedule a time to "do it."

Close by reading James 1:22: "Do not merely listen to the word, and so deceive yourselves. Do what it says."

Then play the game again.

Take-off Time

Activity Level: high

Activity Area: large classroom, gymnasium, or outside

Supplies: two shirts or hats

The Game: If you've always wanted to know what it's like to be an air-traffic controller, playing this game probably won't help—but it's fun, and you can pretend.

Throw two shirts or hats on the ground about six feet apart. This careful positioning represents the aircraft launch area. Have players line up in pairs in a double column behind and at a ninety-degree angle from the launch area (see illustration below).

Have partners choose who will be the airplane and who will be the pilot. Then say: **All airplanes, please close your eyes.**

PAIRS OF KIDS

You must rely on your pilots to direct you by voice commands only—no physical contact, unless a crash is imminent. Airplanes, you have been equipped with high-tech safety bumpers. Please place your hands up, palms out, in front of your face. These bumpers should be up and in use at all altitudes. Pilots, before you are granted your pilot's license, please note that this exercise is designed to build trust. So verbally pilot your aircraft with great care.

Launch a new plane about every five seconds by motioning a pair through the launch area and on to the room or "field." The sighted pilots maneuver their airplanes as carefully or dramatically as the situation and trust level allow. As more and more planes make their way onto and around the field, the opportunity for excitement (and crashes) increases. Remind pilots that if contact with another plane is imminent, they should step in and physically try to prevent a collision.

After all planes and pilots have been launched, begin bringing them back through a new landing strip. Reposition the two shirts or hats in another part of the field. Bring pairs back by calling out the pilot or plane's name, not necessarily in their launch sequence. The idea is to "land" the pairs in rapid succession through the entrance outlined by the shirts or hats so the pilots have to think and react quickly, using only their voices. After all planes have safely landed, have partners switch roles and prepare again for takeoff.

Encourage the planes to make lots of aeronautic noises while zooming around the field. An increasing airborne cacophony adds to the intensity of flight and, more pragmatically, allows the planes to hear nearby aircraft.

Learning Option: Oh Say, Can You See?

Themes: future, trust

Have everyone come in for a landing and a discussion. Ask:
- **What was it like to be a plane? a pilot?**
- **How did it feel to trust a pilot you couldn't see?**
- **How easy or hard was it for pilots to get the planes to trust and follow them?**
- **How was this like trusting in God, whom we can't see?**
- **What do you think it's like for God to get us to trust and follow him?**

Read Jeremiah 29:11-12. Have kids close their eyes and offer a silent prayer for their future, which they can't see.

Then have everyone open their eyes and look around them. Offer a prayer to God for all the blessings they can see.

Walking Trust Circle

Activity Level: medium

Activity Area: large classroom, gymnasium, or outside

Supplies: none

The Game: This trust exercise is potentially the best or not-so-best activity you can present to your group. Do you sense the flashing caution sign? I hope so. Don't present this activity until you're sure the participants care enough about one another to make it work.

Ask the participants to arrange themselves in a circle. Shouldn't be too hard—positioning in a square or pentagon is another matter, but a circle? Child's play.

Once players are standing in a circle, say: **When I give a signal, slowly and carefully walk directly from where you're standing to the opposite side of the circle. We'll move simultaneously. Obviously there'll be some physical contact near circle center, but if everyone is aware of the mass movement and impending melee, the shoulder bumps and palm contact should be no problem. Ready? Walk.**

If everything goes well, ask the players to make another trip across the circle, but at a slightly increased rate of speed. If the first time across presented some problems, discuss those problems before attempting a second crossing.

For a final crossing, have players close their eyes and put "bumpers up." Remember, bumpers up is a hands-up, palms-out, elbows-in position that blindfolded or eyes-closed participants assume to protect their faces and bodies as they sightlessly move about.

Say: **Walking with your eyes closed will present a heavy-duty trust scenario. I'll do my best to protect you from physical hazards during the time that the group's trust is being so obviously displayed. Let other players know where you are as you walk by repeating, "Walking, walking." Ready? Eyes closed, bumpers up.**

Allow enough time for the group to discuss each crossing. Encourage kids to demonstrate compassion toward one another, and ask for willingness to protect one another from the consequences of uncaring contact. Emphasize that speed is not important, compassionate contact is.

*L*earning Opti*o*n: Compassion Action

Themes: care, compassion, servanthood

After the last eyes-closed, bumpers-up attempt, have players open their eyes, lower their bumpers, and sit in a circle. Ask:

● **How did you feel during this game?**

● **How compassionate and caring were you to one another?**

Read Colossians 3:12: "Therefore, as God's chosen people, holy and dearly loved, clothe yourselves with compassion, kindness, humility, gentleness and patience." Ask:

● **What do you think it means to "clothe yourself with compassion"?**

● **Is it easy or hard for you to be compassionate today? Explain.**

● **What is a compassionate thing you can do next week for a family member, a friend, or someone you don't even know?**

After kids share, read Psalm 145:9: "The Lord is good to all; he has compassion on all he has made." Close in prayer by thanking God for his compassion and goodness.

game tip

This game's purpose is to promote caring between participants. The safety of this activity depends entirely upon your "reading" of the group's readiness for controlled participation. Don't use this activity until you judge that the group is experienced enough to jointly handle the responsibility of one another's safety.

urt Rope

Activity Level: medium

Activity Area: large classroom, gymnasium, or outside

Supplies: a sturdy synthetic rope (the length depends on the size of your group)

The Game: Obtain a length of sturdy one-half-inch-wide rope made of a synthetic fiber such as nylon or Dacron. Static rope is best for this tensioned exercise. The length depends on the number of players. A one-hundred-foot-length of rope will allow you to handle a large group. Knot the rope so it forms a circle. Experiment with the knot to be sure it holds under tension.

Place the rope on the ground to form a circle. Ask all the players to stand on the outside of the circled rope and pick it up. Say: **Here's the challenge. Everyone step back until you feel tension in the rope. Stand with your feet about shoulder width apart. Keep holding on to the rope as you start to lean back, slowly bending at the knees until everyone makes posterior contact with the ground at about the same time. One, two, three, sit.**

After congratulating kids on their coordinated landing, ask all the players to try to stand: **One, two, three, stand.**

When the entire group sits, then stands together, everyone develops a sense of teamwork from jointly accomplishing a task.

Variation 1: Try to sit, then stand; take one step to the right; then sit, stand, and take one step to the left. Or use whatever sequence of cooperative movements the group wants to try.

Variation 2: My favorite, with everyone holding the rope in a seated position, is to alternately lean as far forward as possible, then lean back until everyone is lying down. Continue alternating these positions in sequence, like a wave. After about half a dozen trips around the circle, the wave happens spontaneously and rapidly.

Variation 3: Don't use the rope. Have the players stand in a circle, firmly join hands, and take a few baby steps backward until tension is created on everyone's arms. Number off by ones and twos all the way around the circle. Ask all the ones to lean in and the twos to lean out. Then see if everyone can lean back, maintain balance, and sit down together. Have everyone stand together. Then have everyone sit and stand as a wave.

Learning Option: Body of Christ—Teamwork

Themes: body of Christ, teamwork, uniqueness

Use this game to illustrate the principle that each person is needed for the whole group to function as a team.

Read about how the body of Christ works together in 1 Corinthians 12:12-27. Have everyone lean out and freeze in position as you thank God for each person in the circle, each part of the body of Christ.

Brain Stretchers

A Bottleneck

Activity Level: low

Activity Area: anywhere

Supplies: a plastic soda bottle and a plastic pen cap

The Game: Here's an easy-to-set-up, low-on-props, simple-to-explain, and tough-to-figure-out brain game.

Take a large, empty plastic soda bottle (the bigger the better), and put one of those plastic pen caps inside it (you know, the cheap-o pen cap that you remove and seldom use again). Set the bottle upright, and leave the bottle cap off.

Have your group work in pairs to try to solve the puzzle. Ask: **How can you get the pen cap out of the bottle without knocking the bottle over, turning it upside down, or touching it in any way?**

Here's the answer: Pour water into the bottle until the plastic cap floats out. Correct—the pen cap floats!

Learning Option: A Way Out

Theme: temptation

Pour out the water and begin again with the pen cap inside the empty bottle. Fill a pitcher with water.

Give each person a chance to add water to the bottle. At the same time, have the person name one type of no-way-out situation, such as money problems or a large group of friends who are trying to get you to join in drinking.

Have students add water to the bottle as they name situations. When the cap gets close to the top, have someone read 1 Corinthians 10:13: "No temptation has seized you except what is common to man. And God is faithful; he will not let you be tempted beyond what you can bear. But when you are tempted, he will also provide a way out so that you can stand up under it."

Add more water so the pen cap finds a "way out." Close in prayer, thanking God for help in tempting situations.

A Corker

Activity Level: low

Activity Area: anywhere

Supplies: a dime and an empty glass bottle with a cork

The Game: Place a dime inside an empty glass bottle, then replace the cork firmly. Set the bottle in front of the group, and ask: **Without pulling out the cork, breaking the bottle, cutting the glass, melting the glass or burning the cork, how can the dime be removed from inside the bottle?**

Have kids work in pairs to come up with ideas. Some sharpies or instinctive lateral thinkers may get the answer immediately, but most will just look dumbfounded and offer the easy and typical responses: "Must be a trick" or "Can't be done!"

Here's the answer: Push the cork into the bottle.

Learning Option:
God the Ultimate Problem-Solver

Themes: God's power, problems, solving problems

Have kids gather in a circle around the bottle. Give each person a dime. If you're low on cash, have kids supply their own. Ask:

● **When I first told you the problem, who thought it was impossible to solve? Why did it seem impossible?**

● **How did you feel when the problem was solved?**

● **What problems are you facing right now that seem impossible to solve?**

Read Matthew 17:20b-21 and Mark 10:27. Ask:

● **What do these verses say about problem-solving?**

● **How can we rely on God to help us with our problems?**

Offer a time for kids to give their problems to God. Have kids place the dimes in the bottle to represent the problems they're giving to God. Place another cork in the bottle to secure the dimes in the bottle.

Have kids join hands and offer their problems to God in prayer. Agree to meet again in one month. At that time, have kids share the solutions to their problems and push the cork inside the bottle to retrieve the dimes. If some problems are still unanswered, continue to pray.

Aphorism Revision

Activity Level: low

Activity Area: anywhere

Supplies: newsprint, markers, paper, and pencils

The Game: Do you have a favorite aphorism? "What's that?" you might ask. It's a short statement presenting a clever observation or truth. I kind of like "A king unlettered is a donkey crowned," but that somewhat esoteric maxim isn't what we need for this word game. Instead, we need a somewhat well-worn phrase, one most kids would know.

How about "A stitch in time saves nine"?

Write an aphorism on newsprint. Vary the types of letters you use (uppercase, lowercase, printed, cursive) and leave out any punctuation—we don't want to make it too easy. Split the letters into groups that look like words.

For example, if you're using "A stitch in time saves nine," it might look something like this:

aS titCh iNti mE sav Esn iNE

Have players form groups of four. Present the aphorism you've written, and have players work within their groups to sort out the letters and come up with the right phrase.

Next give each group a sheet of paper and a pencil. Have each group choose a favorite aphorism and write it creatively on the paper—using uppercase letters, lowercase letters, cursive, unique spacing, no punctuation, and so on.

Once aphorisms are complete, have groups switch papers with each other and try to identify the aphorisms written on them. Once groups guess the aphorisms, they can write new ones and switch papers again.

ifit sWoR thdoi *n*gi Tswor thO verd oinG

Need a jump-start on aphorisms? Try these:

i ts*a* l **O**ngla neth *a*thas *not* urnin*g*

It's a long lane that has no turning.

ra ts*l* ea v**e**a*s* inki ngs h*i*p

Rats leave a sinking ship.

t**r**u sti so bvio us aft **e** ritsd isc ov er*y*

Trust is obvious after its discovery.

*t*h **e**b ig g**e**r *the* ya r**e**theh ard**e**rt *h***e**yfa*ll*

The bigger they are, the harder they fall.

*a*l lswe l*lt* h*a*t**e** ndsw *e* ll

All's well that ends well.

d**O**as *u* a*y*a ndn**O**t asid**O**

Do as I say and not as I do.

st*i* ll*w* a ters *ru* nde ep

Still waters run deep.

Variation: When a group figures out an aphorism, have the group decide how to mime it, not tell it, to the other groups. For example, for "Still waters run deep," players could mime still, deep water by moving their hands in a slight flowing motion above their heads. Another group member could pretend to swim along at their feet.

*L*earning Opti*o*n: Proverbial Sayings

Themes: Proverbs, wisdom

Have players stay in their groups of four, and give each group a Bible and a fresh sheet of paper. Have the groups turn to the book of Proverbs—a book filled with aphorisms.

Play the game again, and this time have each group choose a verse in Proverbs to write in a unique way. Then have groups switch papers and decipher the Proverbs. For example, a group might write Proverbs 17:17 as

αf**R**i En dlov e**S** αtal Lt**i** m**e**sa n D**a**b rot HeR**i** sBo rn**F** or **A**d versi *ty*

A friend loves at all times, and a brother is born for adversity.

or Proverbs 27:19 as

aswa Terre f**L**e Cts *afa* C**e**so amAn shEar tr**e** FlEc tst h**EM** an

As water reflects a face, so a man's heart reflects the man.

If you want to include your entire church family in the fun, give each group of students a long sheet of newsprint and markers. Have each group write its proverb with its unique spacing on the newsprint. Then hang the proverbs in the church hallways for members of the congregation to discover and decipher.

It's All in the Straw

Activity Level: low

Activity Area: anywhere

Supplies: an empty, eight- to twelve-ounce glass bottle with a somewhat narrow neck (such as a juice or soft drink bottle); a plastic straw; and a towel

The Game: You love these easy-to-set-up, low-on-props, simple-to-explain, and tough-to-figure-out brain games; I know you do. Try this one.

Lay down a towel, and place an empty eight- to twelve-ounce glass bottle on it. Place a plastic straw by the bottle.

Say: **Here's the problem. Figure out how to hold the bottle off the floor for five seconds. You can use only the straw—glue, rubber bands, or anything else is not allowed. You can't tie a knot in the straw either.**

Have kids work in pairs to solve the brain game.

Here's how to do it: Bend the straw sharply about one-third of the way down its length. Stick the one-third portion of the straw into the mouth of the bottle until the bent part flips partially open and jams itself against the interior shoulder of the bottle. Lift the protruding end of the straw, and the bottle follows. Easy!

game tip

A hefty milkshake type of straw works best for this brain game. Also, just in case your lifting plan doesn't fly, the towel underneath the bottle will cushion the fall.

Learning Option: Impossible

Themes: God's power, obstacles

Gather kids around the bottle and the straw. Say: **At first, it seemed impossible to lift the bottle off the ground with just a straw. But then someone figured it out, and the impossible was made possible.**

Have kids form four groups, and give each group one of these passages to read: Matthew 9:1-8 (Jesus heals a paralyzed man); Mark 6:45-51 (Jesus walks on water); Luke 7:11-16 (Jesus brings a man back to life); John 6:1-13 (Jesus feeds five thousand people). Ask:

● **What seemingly impossible thing did Jesus do in the passage you read?**

● **How was the impossible made possible?**

Read aloud: **"All things are possible with God" (Mark 10:27b).**

Have each person share one thing in life that at first looked impossible but with God became possible. For example, maybe a sick relative got better, or a long-lost friend who had moved away returned after several years.

Have kids take turns holding up the bottle by the straw and saying quickly, "God can do all things." After everyone has had a turn, close in prayer, thanking God for making the impossible possible.

It's Amazing

Activity Level: low

Activity Area: anywhere

Supplies: a sheet of paper and a pencil for each player, and at least one calculator

The Game: When I was in school, I used to have bad dreams about arithmetic, algebra, and geometry. The dreams were justified because I didn't do well in classes that had anything to do with numbers. I assume that's why the following numbers game fascinates me. I don't understand how the idea could possibly work. It's amazing.

Give each player a sheet of paper and a pencil. Give these instructions: **Write down your house or apartment number and double it.** (My house number is 9, so we're looking at 18.) **Add 5.** (I can do that: 23.) **Multiply that number by half a hundred.** (23 X 50 = 1150. I used a calculator.) **Add your age.** (Wow, this problem is timeless. That's 1150 + 60 = 1210.) **Now add the number of days in a year** (1210 + 365 = 1575), **and subtract 615** (1575 - 615 = 960). **The last figures of your answer will be your age** (60), **and the first part of the answer** (9) **is your house number.**

It's amazing. Right again.

Have players create their own numbers games. Then have them exchange games and cooperate to figure them out. The fun never ends.

Learning Option: God's So Amazing

Themes: God's power, our amazing God

After playing this numbers game, ask kids: **What did you think is the most amazing thing about this game?**

Say: **God's pretty amazing too. Listen to this verse: "God, how wonderful you are! You are more splendid than the hills full of animals"** (Psalm 76:4, NCV).

Let's express to God our amazement at the wonderful things he has done. Let's each complete this sentence

prayer, one at a time: "God, how wonderful you are! You are more splendid than..." Add what you want to thank God for. For example, you might thank God for the stars and moon at night, the sandy beach, or the majestic mountains. Everyone express your own amazement.

After everyone has completed the sentence prayer, close by reading Psalm 76:4 again. Amazing!

Nocturnal News

Activity Level: low

Activity Area: outside at night (or in a dark area indoors)

Supplies: one large flashlight, three pocket-size mirrors, a newspaper article, and four thumbtacks for every group of five

The Game: The object of this game is for participants to read their assigned newspaper articles. Not so hard, it would seem, until you consider that the article must be read in the dark. Considering the nocturnal essence of the challenge, it's probably best to present this challenge at night.

Prior to the game, use thumbtacks to tack a newspaper article to a tree trunk at about eye level. For every group of five kids, you'll need one article tacked to its own tree trunk.

Have kids form groups of five, then give each group one flashlight and three pocket-size mirrors. Present the challenge by saying: **Your group's job is to read a newspaper article that's attached to a tree trunk. The problem is, the flashlight beam can't be used to directly illuminate the article, nor can the flashlight be taken into the 180-degree area on the newspaper-article side of the tree. Only one mirror is allowed inside this 180-degree area. The other two mirrors can be located anywhere outside that 180-degree area and at least fifteen feet from the tree. The light must be reflected from all three mirrors before it illuminates the paper.** (See the illustration on page 50 for the answer to this challenge.)

game tip

If you're doing this game indoors, simply substitute a piece of furniture or some other object for the tree trunk, and adjust the fifteen-feet-from-the-tree rule as necessary.

game tip

Provide flashlights with strong beams for this game. It's frustrating to attempt to bounce light from mirror to mirror when the light is dim. Dim light = dim interest.

*L*earning Opti*o*n:
Pick the Topic

Theme: anything, becoming like Jesus, God's glory

Adapt this game by finding interesting articles that will lead into your chosen study—articles about kids who've helped people in distress; articles about earthquakes, floods, and famines; or articles about controversial court decisions, for example.

If you want to lead a discussion straight out of the game, you may want to talk about the idea that as people become more like Jesus, they reflect his glory to others. That light is passed on, and tasks or ministries are fulfilled in Jesus' name.

Oh, Wow!

Activity Level: low

Activity Area: anywhere

Supplies: none

The Game: This game really baffled me at first, which isn't saying much when you consider that I'm easily baffled. But quick, here's the answer before I forget...and the problem, too.

Through a series of seemingly indecipherable sounds and hand movements, indicate to an "in-the-know" compatriot a well-known phrase or the name of a famous person. Follow the rules below to communicate your message. The group's challenge is to figure out how this communication is achieved. Here's how:

● Communicate consonants by starting a sentence (any sentence) with the consonant in question. For example, if you were trying to communicate the name "Jesus," you'd start a sentence with the letter J. For example, you might say, "Just listen carefully."

● Communicate vowels by flashing your fingers to indicate a number between one and five that corresponds to the correct vowel:

- ● one finger = a
- ● two fingers = e
- ● three fingers = i
- ● four fingers = o
- ● five fingers = u

The next letter in "Jesus" is "e," so you'd hold up two fingers.

The next letter is "s," so you'd start a sentence with the letter "s." For example, you might say, "Suppose we stop here."

The next letter is "u," so hold up five fingers.

The final letter is "s," so start a sentence with "s." For example, you might say, "Seems OK to me."

● If you choose to communicate more than one word to your partner, say, "Oh, wow!" to indicate the end of a word and the beginning of another. So if you wanted to communicate "Jesus Christ," after the "Seems OK to me" sentence, you'd say, "Oh, wow!" and start another sentence with C. For example, that sentence might be "Come here and listen."

So to sum up the skills, communicating "Jesus Christ" might look and sound like this:

"Just listen carefully." Hold up two fingers. "Suppose we stop here." Hold up five fingers. "Seems OK to me. Oh, wow! Come here and listen. Have you had enough? Repeat that, please." Hold up three fingers. "Sit down. The end."

Now that you've mastered the skills necessary for this game, have a volunteer whisper a name or phrase to you, then communicate it to your partner. Watch the group's amazement when your partner understands what you've crazily communicated.

Obviously, you and your partner need to practice this interplay beforehand, but when it's done well, the hand-and-sound communication is brilliant and almost impossible to decipher. This is just the right activity for a campfire or a rainy day.

Learning Option: Communicating the Gospel

Themes: communication, God's love, God's Word, sharing faith

As a final phrase in the game, communicate this to your partner:

"Communicate the gospel."

After your partner reveals what you said, ask the group:

● **What was it like not knowing what I said in this game?**

● **Would it be possible to communicate the gospel to others using these sounds and hand signals? Explain.**

If kids haven't figured it out already, show everyone how you communicated with your partner. Then use the sound-and-hand communication to tell the group this phrase:

"Spread God's Word."

Ask:

● **What was it like to play this game now that you understand what I was trying to communicate?**

● **How is this like the way we should share our faith with others? How is it different?**

Read Matthew 28:19-20. Then ask:

● **How can we spread God's Word so others understand?**

Close in prayer, asking God for help in spreading God's love.

Communication Builders

Rope Script

Activity Level: low

Activity Area: large classroom, gymnasium, or outside

Supplies: two fifty-foot-lengths of pliable, supple rope or string

The Game: Form two groups...
Let's take a moment to do that.

Most "you-go-here, you-go-there" group divisions end up representing a kind of sociogram. You know, the best athletes or best friends choose up sides, and guess who gets picked last? Halving the group can be fun. Try this:

Ask all players to fold their arms, just as many individuals probably are already doing. All those with their right arms on top are in one group, and those with their left arms on top are in the other group.

There's your split, and if it's not absolutely accurate, just ask a couple of players from one group to join the other group. There's always someone who's ready to jump ship.

Give each group a fifty-foot length of supple rope or string. Say: **In a minute, I'll name a topic, such as "a book name." Huddle as a group to decide what you want to communicate. Then use your rope to spell out the name in cursive. No one in either group is allowed to speak or spell out words with your hands or signal what your group is trying to communicate. Your group can use only the rope. It's up to your group to decide how many players actually manipulate the rope, and how many players concurrently attempt to figure out**

game *tip*

Groups of twenty or more usually end up with almost an even fifty-fifty split. Arm-folding is a genetic trait and is done consistently the same way every time by an individual. For fun, ask all the players to fold their arms with the other arm on top. Kinda makes you wonder about the other group, eh? I mean, it feels so weird.

53

what the other group is trying to communicate. If you think you know what the other group is spelling, wave your hand frantically, and I'll call on you for your response.

Try these topics, and use some of your own: name of a book, name of a movie, name of a movie star, type of Italian food, type of soft drink, flavor of ice cream, type of car, something with wheels, and so on.

Move on to a new topic when someone deciphers a group's message or if somebody gets a mental rope burn.

*L*earning Opti*o*n: A Closing Word of Thanks

Themes: praise, thanks

As the last scripting exercise of the game, have teams script something they are thankful to God for. Once the words have been guessed, have kids join hands and form a circle, then have each person thank God for one thing. Close by thanking God for the gift of voices for offering praise.

Rug Rats

Activity Level: high

Activity Area: large classroom or gymnasium

Supplies: one carpet sample for each person

The Game: Get yourself down to the local carpet store, and ask if they sell carpet samples or carpet remnants. The store folks keep them around to show buyers the look and feel of available styles. I recently bought twenty of these pieces for seventy-five cents each. And there's always the possibility that stores will want to give these samples to you as a charitable donation.

Here's what to do with your newly purchased or donated carpet samples, besides passing them out to friends to use as car mats.

Gather all players at one end of a large, empty classroom or gymnasium. Give one carpet sample to each player. Say: **The floor is covered with sole acid, which dissolves the bottom of your shoes—terrible stuff. Using the carpet samples as steppingstones, work together to get everyone to the opposite wall in the quickest, most efficient way. If anyone slips off or steps off a carpet sample, that person must return to the starting point and begin again. The rugs can move only forward and can't be taken back to the start.**

If your room's floor is polished wood or some other smooth surface, someone will discover that the quickest and most efficient way across is to turn the carpet samples into floor skates. If your floor is made of a rubberized material or carpet, forget the floor skates, and come up with another plan!

Learning Option: The Narrow Road

Themes: Christian life, heaven

Play the game again with no rules. Kids can just run from one side of the gym to the other. Then play a final time with the rug sections as described earlier.

Afterward, ask everyone to gather around for a quick Bible study. Have them sit on their carpet samples. Ask:

● **What was it like to run with no rules?**

● **What was it like using the carpet samples and following all those rules?**

Read Matthew 7:13-14: "Enter through the narrow gate. For wide is the gate and broad is the road that leads to destruction, and many enter through it. But small is the gate and narrow the road that leads to life, and only a few find it." Ask:

● **How was the game with no rules like the broad road?**

● **How was using the carpet samples and following the rules like the narrow road?**

● **Why is it easier to run with no rules?**

● **What are the rewards for following the narrow road?**

● **How did you help each other complete the course with the carpet samples?**

● **How is this like the way we help each other stay on the right path in everyday life?**

● **How can you help each other to follow the narrow road this week?**

Close by asking kids to stack the carpet samples. As kids place their carpet samples in a pile, have them share how they'll help others follow the narrow road that leads to God's kingdom.

Save the City

Activity Level: high

Activity Area: gymnasium

Supplies: a plastic gallon-sized milk carton (with the bottom cut off) for each person, lots of tennis balls, and some obstacles (such as furniture)

The Game: During this game, players communicate with each other to find the best and quickest way to "save the city." The object of the game is to transport radioactive isotopes (tennis balls) to a destination without letting the isotopes touch the floor. If an isotope touches the floor, it reverses the ionization of the subfloor rebars, resulting in a decomposition of structural integrity and collapse of the horizontal supporting mechanism (floor). Also, radioactive isotopes *must not* touch any body part...I won't go into detail about the anatomical consequences—too brutal.

It's your group's civic and humanitarian responsibility to use the available customized lead shield transporters (plastic gallon-sized milk cartons with the bottoms cut off) to transport the isotopes up, over, and across a few well-chosen obstacles.

Gather the isotopes on one side of the room. Designate the opposite side of the room as the destination for the isotopes. (The more tennis balls, the more action.) Have each player choose a place to stand between the two sides. The more obstacles, the better. Players can stand on table tops, couches, chairs—you name it.

Say: **Every isotope must make contact with the interior of each transporter. (Translation: The tennis balls must be transported from carton to carton.) You must remain in your positions. You can move by pivoting on one foot. Communicate with one another. Encourage one another to move quickly. We'll time our first attempt, then we'll play again and try to beat our time. Transporters ready? Begin.**

> **game tip**
>
> Have players supply their own decorated isotope transporters (to keep you from having to slice up *beaucoup* milk cartons).

Variation 1: Play this as a large group and compete against your own times, or form teams and try to beat each other's times.

Variation 2: Color a few tennis balls, and indicate that the colored ones are particularly hot isotopes and can stay in a transporter for a maximum of five seconds. After that, a transporter meltdown will occur. Terrible thing to see. Don't let it happen.

Learning Option: Spread Your Faith Around

Themes: faith, obstacles, sharing faith

Play the game again, imagining that the tennis balls are "faith" and kids are spreading their faith to others. Afterward, ask:
- **What did you find easiest or hardest about the game?**
- **What was it like to imagine you were spreading your faith to others?**
- **What obstacles were in your way in the game?**
- **What obstacles are in your way when you share your faith in real life?**

Have kids gather in a circle, and collect all the game equipment. Affirm the person on your right by describing that person's faith by using a word that begins with that person's first initial. For example, you might say, "Bob, you have a beautiful faith." Bob then affirms the next person: "Dan, you have a dynamic faith." Dan affirms the next person: "Amanda, you have an amazing faith." Continue until everyone has been affirmed. Close with prayer, asking God to help kids spread their faith to others.

Sense of Rumor

Activity Level: low

Activity Area: large classroom or gymnasium

Supplies: none

The Game: The goal of this game is to pass a message from one end of a line to the other by pantomiming a simple scenario.

Ask participants to line up, single file, facing the back of the person in front of them. Stand at the back of the line, where you'll be the first person to create a pantomimed message. Tap the person in front of you. That person will turn around to look at you (everyone else is still looking away). Pantomime a short description of a commonplace action (for example, making and eating a peanut butter and jelly sandwich or filling a car with gas, washing the windows, and paying the attendant).

The person who just saw the pantomime taps the shoulder of the next person in line, who turns around and views the pantomimed message. This manic miming continues until the final person in line receives the message and pantomimes his or her interpretation to the rest of the group. Then you can show your original pantomime.

Have players take turns "starting the rumors."

Prepare yourself for some bizarre changes in meaning and a considerable amount of humor. Let everyone have a chance to stand at the back of the line and start a pantomimed message. Watch the rumors spread.

Variation 1: If you have a large group, form two single-file lines of participants leading away from your position at the apex of a V, with everyone in the two lines also facing away from you. (See the illustration on the following page.)

game tip

As the game progresses, or if your group gets good at this game, try introducing some more complex pantomime scenarios. For example, a person drives to the store, buys some potato chips, munches a few chips while driving home, turns on the television, and watches a soap opera in a most becoming couch-potato fashion.

variation 1

Tap the shoulders of the two people closest to you in the V. They'll turn around and observe your pantomimed message, then turn back to their initial positions and signal to the next people to view their impression of your mimed message.

When the last two participants have seen the pantomime, they demonstrate their version of the message. Then it's your turn to show the group what you initially mimed. Remember, they aren't laughing at you, but at the situation.

Variation 2: To accommodate more people, form more than two single-file lines leading away from you, like spokes around a wheel. Or set up four lines as a W, with you standing in a central position (see illustration below).

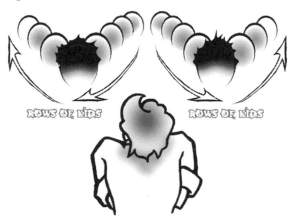

variation 2

The final four players eventually demonstrate to the entire group what's been passed along to them and is now so vastly different.

Variation 3: If your players get really good at this game and you want to complicate it for more laughs, have players reverse the message at some point during transmittal. In other words, after the message has been sent and several players have pantomimed it, have one player try to pantomime the actions in reverse and pass it along that way.

To make it really complicated, have another player at some point try to reverse the message again, putting the actions in their original order.

*L*earning Opti○n: Guarding the Tongue

Themes: gossip, put-downs, rumors, speech

Wrap up Sense of Rumor by having kids take turns reading Scriptures that deal with guarding the tongue. There's a lot to choose from. Who knew the tongue was such a powerful weapon? Ask kids to read as many of these passages as they can until their tongues get tired: Psalm 5:9; 10:7; 12:3-4; 50:19; 52:2-4; Proverbs 6:16-19; 10:31; 17:4, 20; 25:23; 26:28; James 3:3-12.

You might have kids play Sense of Rumor again, this time pantomiming the messages of these Scripture passages. Then encourage kids to discuss ways to deal with gossip, put-downs, and other negative habits of speech. Ask questions like these:

● **Why do you think it's so important to watch what we say?**

● **Why are gossip and put-downs so tempting?**

● **What are some ways we can avoid the temptation to gossip, put others down, or say other negative things?**

Win-Win, or What?

Activity Level: high

Activity Area: gymnasium or outside

Supplies: tape or rope to define a line in the playing area

The Game: Use tape or rope to mark a ten- to fifteen-foot line on the gym floor or ground.

Have kids form two groups, and have them stand on either side of the line. **Say: You have two minutes to get as many players as possible from the other side of the line to commit to being on your side. This can be accomplished by compassionate force (dragging but no punching or pinching), compelling conviction ("You'd better get over here"), or win-win cajoling ("If you come over here this time, I'll go over there next time"). Once someone is on your side of the line, they don't have to stay. If someone drags you across the line, you're free to return to the other side. Go!**

Be available to interpret the compassion and temper the compelling, making sure players don't get out of hand.

Players will probably figure out that the best way to win this game is to talk with each other, deciding on some kind of solution so that everyone agrees and everyone wins.

game tip

To create a quality line, purchase gray caulking pipe. It's a flexible, rod-like product used for stuffing into cracks that are too large for semifluid caulk. It comes in a variety of diameters to fill cracks of various sizes. Get a section of 3/8-inch-diameter caulking pipe, and secure it to the floor with tape, or attach it to the ground with two or three 3/8-inch staples. Your players will be impressed with your aesthetic approach to play.

Learning Option: Drawing Others to Christ

Themes: hypocrisy, integrity, sharing faith, showing faith

When all is said and dragged, settle down for a discussion. Ask:

● **What is "win-win," anyway?**

● **Why did you choose the technique you used? Was it effective?**

- **If everyone ended up on one side, was that satisfying to everyone? Explain.**
- **Is straddling the line at the end of two minutes an alternative? Why or why not?**
- **How was this game like trying to share your faith to introduce other people to Christ?**
- **How was straddling the line in the game like straddling the line between Christianity and the world?**
- **Apart from the pulling and dragging that occurred in the game, what real-life actions would help draw others to Christ?**

Read Colossians 3:12-14. Have everyone reflect on these win-win actions: showing compassion; being kind, humble, gentle and patient; getting along with one another; forgiving one another; loving one another.

Have each person choose one win-win action to try over the next week. Encourage kids to invite others to come to the next church activity with them.

Group Challenges

Bizarre Boccie

Activity Level: high

Activity Area: outside

Supplies: two Boccie or croquet balls for every player and a one-inch wooden or plastic ball (or a golf ball) for every four or five players

The Game: I've never played a game of real Boccie, but I consider myself an above-average player of Bizarre Boccie. Here's what you need to play.

Each player will need two colored Boccie balls. Don't buy the professional Boccie balls, because they're extremely expensive and absolutely unnecessary. Just buy the inexpensive backyard variety, or get a set of old croquet balls. Each group of four or five players will need a one-inch wooden or plastic ball (or a golf ball) to serve as a jack.

Go outside anywhere to play this game. The more fences, streams, roads, gullies, trees, and other obstacles, the better.

Have groups of four or five spread out to their own playing areas. Players decide who goes first in their group. They can flip a coin or just say, "I'll go first" or "You go first." Whoever goes first (called the pelota person or PP for short) throws the jack. The jack acts as a target for all incoming Boccie balls.

Then the PP decides how the balls are to be propelled toward the jack. Therein lies the bizarre aspect of the game, the big variation from regular Boccie—all the players must follow the style of the PP's throw. The scoring details follow.

● **One point:** the closest propelled Boccie ball to the jack (where the ball ends up, not where it first makes contact)

● **One point:** if a Boccie ball hits the jack

● **Three points:** if both of a player's Boccie balls end up closest to the jack

● **Five points:** if a ball ends up less than a thumb's width from the jack

Group members can throw their Boccie balls one at a time or

all at once; it's up to the PP. Here are some bizarre throws for PPs to attempt. Let me tell my favorite example first. As the designated PP, it's my turn. I mark a starting line in the ground or dirt. I casually flip the jack about fifteen feet away. Next, I tuck my two Boccie balls into the fleshy area just above my collarbone (clavicle, for you premed students). I hold the Boccie balls in place by scrunching my shoulders, thus pressing the balls against my neck. To "throw" them (both at once, obviously), I get a running start of a few feet and shout, *"Olé!"* I drop my shoulders, allowing the Boccie balls to continue forward as I come to a screeching halt just behind the line.

After all group members copy my throw and all Boccie balls are lying on the ground, all points are added up. Then the next PP demonstrates a new delivery system that's even more wildly creative than the just-tried "el toro" technique. Here are some more ideas:

● The PP throws the jack, stands with his or her back toward the jack, looks over his or her shoulder for a last glance, then delivers one Boccie ball backward to where he or she thinks the jack is located. Then the PP delivers his or her second Boccie ball in the same manner. All group members then copy the delivery. Add up the points!

● The PP drops the jack at his or her feet. Then all throwers cluster so they're standing back-to-back and shoulder-to-shoulder. They yell, "One, two, three," and loft their Boccie balls (both at once) overhead, then vacate where they were standing. In other words, get outta there before the Boccie balls come down to earth. See where they land, and add up the points.

● The PP throws the jack at least twenty-five feet away, then propels one Boccie ball at a time as you would in a shot put.

● The PP looks out over the terrain for any features that would make the game more difficult. For example, the PP could toss the jack so it comes to rest on an incline. When Boccie balls roll up the incline, they invariably roll down. Who can get closest to the jack?

● The PP tosses the jack about twenty feet away. The PP holds a Boccie ball behind his or her back with both hands, leans well forward, then flips the ball forward, up and over his or her head.

● The PP identifies an area to throw the Boccie ball over or through, such as the fork of a tree, the handle of a lawn mower, or a clothesline. The PP places the jack beyond that area. If a thrown Boccie ball does not pass over or through the area on its way toward the jack, the throw is forfeit.

● The PP places the jack immediately in front of a wall and stipulates that if the wall is hit by a Boccie ball, the throw is forfeit.

Encourage all Bizarre Boccie players to take turns being the PP and creating their own bizarre throws. It's wild.

Learning Option: Onward Toward the Goal

Themes: eternal life, goals, grace, heaven

After a rousing game of Bizarre Boccie, have players sit in a circle for a well-deserved rest. Have someone read Philippians 3:13b-14, 17: "But one thing I do: Forgetting what is behind and straining toward what is ahead, I press on toward the goal to win the prize for which God has called me heavenward in Christ Jesus. Join with others in following my example, brothers, and take note of those who live according to the pattern we gave you."

Ask:

● **What does it mean to "forget what is behind and strain toward what is ahead"?**

● **How does our past sometimes weigh us down and keep us from going forward?**

● **What is "the prize for which God has called me heavenward in Christ Jesus"?**

● **Whose example are we to follow as we live life?**

Play another round of Bizarre Boccie, with you acting as the PP for the entire group. Have all the players imitate your throw. Before they throw, have them silently offer up something from their past that they want to let go of so they can go forward toward the goal.

After everyone has thrown, join hands for prayer. Ask for God's help to imitate Christ, and thank him that, through his grace, we can reach the "goal" of eternal life.

Can Do

Activity Level: medium

Activity Area: outside

Supplies: an empty aluminum soft drink can, a Swiss army knife can opener or a P-38, a sharp knife (such as an X-Acto knife), and an emery board

The Game: Ever played with a reamed and truncated soft drink can? The object of this game is to hold an empty and altered pop can and, using a spiral football-like throw, cause that ultra-lightweight piece of aluminum to fly fifty feet or so.

Find an empty aluminum can, and remove the end with the pop-top. You might get lucky and find a can opener that works, but each time I've spontaneously fashioned a Can Do in the field, the kitchen-type can openers available just haven't cut deep enough to do the job. Don't despair; there are a couple of tools that work.

If you were once in the military or have done some camping, you might be familiar with a small piece of folding metal called a P-38. (I have no idea what the P or 38 stands for, but I do know that it does a bang-up job of removing can tops, specifically tops of soft drink cans.) Otherwise, the old Swiss army knife can opener also gets the job done.

After you've removed the top, use a sharp knife (an X-Acto knife works really well) to cut the can in half, maintaining its cylindrical shape. You'll use only the top half of the can for this game.

Cutting out the top and cutting the can in half shouldn't take more than a couple of minutes. Cutting aluminum is not difficult, just different. Total cost—*nada*.

Use an emery board to smooth out any jagged edges. (See the illustration on the following page.)

> **game tip**
>
> Make several Can Dos so as many participants as possible can play at a time. Have kids form teams for distance throws, partner passing, or Can Do-throwing relay races. The FUNN never ends.

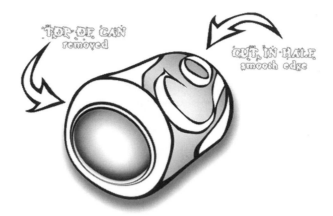

TOP OF CAN
removed

CUT IN HALF
smooth edge

Work's over—it's FUNN time (Functional Understanding's Not Necessary)! Take that hollow piece of potential trash outside and chuck it toward your group, remembering to spiral it like a football and to keep the top of the can forward as you throw. Experiment a bit with your throwing technique because the flight characteristics of a Can Do aren't immediately predictable—it'll sail and spin left, right, up, and down for no apparent reason. But sail it does, amidst exclamations of "Wow! That's neat! Lemme try!"

When everyone is reasonably adept at throwing the Can Do, set up the challenge. Select a target in your playing area (such as a tree or a flagpole), and have kids take turns throwing the Can Do at the target to see how many times they can hit it. Or have players take turns throwing the Can Do to see who can set a distance record for one Can Do flight.

Just another excuse to throw something and have some FUNN.

Learning Option: Confidence With Christ

Themes: confidence, goals, God's power

Gather all Can Do players, and read the following passage: "I can do everything through him who gives me strength" (Philippians 4:13).

Have every player find a partner. Have partners tell each other a goal or a situation they're struggling with. Maybe it's a paper to write, a test to take, a parent to forgive, or a friend to confront. After everyone has shared, have kids take turns throwing the Can Do. As each person throws, have him or her offer the struggle up to God, either silently or aloud. After each throw, have everyone repeat aloud: "I can do everything through him who gives me strength."

FFEACH

Activity Level: medium

Activity Area: anywhere

Supplies: a stopwatch

The Game: An old playmate of mine, Steve Butler, invented and regularly plays a pantomime game called FFEACH, pronounced "feech." FFEACH is an acronym for fast foods, electrical appliances, and comic book heroes. (I guess you could put the "b" in there for "book," but it messes up the pronunciation. FFEACBH doesn't sound like much.) For unbridled intensity coupled with fast thinking and action, this activity is hard to beat.

To play, have kids form groups of five to seven players, and separate them by a few yards. Situate yourself somewhat away from and between the groups (see illustration below).

Announce to the groups that you'll all choose a topic together: fast foods, electrical appliances, or comic book heroes. Then each group will send a player to you, and you'll secretly and separately assign a different item within that topic to each of them.

Those players must swiftly return to their groups and act out (nonverbal but helpful sounds can be made) their specific item to their waiting and ultra-attentive team members. As soon as they guess the item, another group member dashes up to receive a new assignment. Here are the topics and some examples of items within those topics:

● fast foods (examples: cheeseburger, fries, shake)

● electrical appliances (examples: blender, vacuum, can opener)

● comic book heroes (examples: Superman, Spider Man, Sonic)

Time the teams, and keep track of how long it takes each one to guess an item for every player on the team. Tell kids that the first team to correctly guess an item for each player has set a new world record. Then the group at large can choose a different topic and continue playing in an effort to beat the world record.

If win-lose world records seem inappropriate or unacceptable for your group, ask the first team finished to hurry over to another frantically miming group to offer its world-class expertise. In this way, the groups are not competing against one another, but rather against themselves. Groups can help other groups only by miming.

Variation: Gloree Rohnke, my wife and permanent playmate, developed an interesting and entertaining variation of FFEACH called MOOCH (movies, occupations, and hums). This game is played identically to FFEACH, except that the topics are different and players have the option of acting out or humming whatever tunes you've chosen. Choose tunes that apply to the age level of your group. Humming "Green Eyes" to a high school youth group works about as well as humming rap songs to a retirement-community gathering.

Humming while you're laughing or trying to be serious causes giggles all around.

game tip

It's important for the facilitator to either keep a written list of items within topics or to have played the game often enough to be able to quickly recall items within topics. As the game intensifies, players will probably come up to you in twos and threes eagerly—no—frantically anticipating their miming task. Few games create such intensity on the faces of the players—good photographic stuff.

Learning Option: Bible BIMP

Themes: anything, the Bible

We have to have a Bible game along this same line—the Bible is filled with topics just waiting to be mimed. Try playing BIMP (books, individuals, miracles, parables). Choose a topic related to what your group is studying, then have teams mime items within that topic. Here are some examples:

● books: Genesis, Exodus, Leviticus, Matthew, Mark, Luke, John—you have lots to choose from

● individuals: Go for well-known ones, such as Moses, Mary, or Joseph; then try lesser-known ones, such as Deborah and Methuselah.

● miracles: crossing the Red Sea, manna from heaven, feeding the five thousand, raising Lazarus

● parables: a tiny mustard seed of faith, the sower, the good Samaritan

This game is played like FFEACH and MOOCH, with different topic headings. Instead of miming the books of the Bible, participants could hum the alphabet song and stop at the appropriate letter, doing so until they hum and spell the book title.

Don't settle for BIMP; have players make up a new name and go for new topics. There's a lot to study within that book!

Fifteen Ball

Activity Level: high

Activity Area: gymnasium or outside

Supplies: one inflated beach ball, one fifteen-foot rope, and two supports (such as trees, poles, or walls) for the rope

The Game: This is a game requiring minimal rules, few skills, no teams, maximum cooperation, high energy, play by choice, and inexpensive props. It's a great icebreaker for everyone. Sounds like a winner, and it is.

Before the game, tie a rope between two supports (trees, poles, walls) horizontally fifteen feet from the ground.

Hold up an inflated beach ball and say: **The object of this game is to hit this ball over the fifteen-foot-high rope and end up with fifteen points. You get one point every time the ball goes over the rope, unless you kick it over or hit it over with your head. Then you get two or three points, respectively. You are all on the same team and can play any position you like. In fact, I encourage you to change sides by moving back and forth under the rope.**

Here are a few more rules:

● The ball can be hit as many times as desired before it goes over the rope, but the same person can't hit it twice in a row.

● If the ball hits the ground, all accumulated points are lost.

● Catching or palming the ball isn't allowed, but the ball can be struck, smacked, or kicked with any part of the body.

Learning Option: Higher Thoughts

Themes: focusing on God, God's power, our amazing God, wisdom

After the fifteenth point is attained, hold on to the beach ball and gather kids in a circle under the rope. Read Isaiah 55:9: "As the heavens are higher than the earth, so are my ways higher than your ways and my thoughts than your thoughts." Ask:

● **What does this mean: God's ways are higher than our ways? What are God's ways? What are our ways?**

● **What does this mean: God's thoughts are higher than our thoughts? What are God's thoughts? What are our thoughts?**

● **Why is it so easy to look down—at ourselves, our lives, and our problems?**

● **How can we keep looking up—focusing our eyes on God's ways and thoughts?**

Play the game again. Each time the ball goes over the high rope, have everyone shout, "Look up!"

Frantic

Activity Level: high

Activity Area: gymnasium

Supplies: one tennis ball for each person, fifteen extra tennis balls, one whistle, and one stopwatch

The Game: The ideal Frantic court has nothing around the edges, such as bleachers, chairs, or stacked mats. So clear the playing area as much as possible.

Place one tennis ball (rabid nugget) per player right smack in the center of the gym. Most gyms have a circle in the center. If not, just cluster the tennis balls somewhere near the center. (Frantic is not a sanctioned Olympic sport, so you can fudge a little.)

Everyone is on the same team and is competing against the clock, so have a stopwatch ready. Players position themselves anywhere on the court they want to. (Is that empowering, or what?) Use the side of your foot in a sweeping motion to kick the cluster of rabid nuggets. As you kick the cluster, start the stopwatch.

With all the rabid nuggets suddenly rolling everywhere, it becomes the team's task to keep them moving. Players can kick the rabid nuggets with their feet; no hands are allowed. If a nugget rolls to a stop, the team receives a "berserk," which is a loud whistle blow.

After the sixth berserk (or whistle blow), stop the clock and record the time. That time represents the team's first "frenzy."

Cluster the rabid nuggets for another attempt. This second attempt is significant because the team members have the opportunity to use their mutual experience to improve upon the first try. Make sure you give the group enough time and encouragement to talk about what they did and what they can do to improve their time.

Here are some more rules:

● A rabid nugget must be restarted if it comes to a stop. If after five seconds the rabid nugget has not been restarted, a second berserk is issued.

● Add complexity to each frenzy by rolling another rabid nugget into play every ten seconds.

● If a rabid nugget becomes inadvertently lodged behind or next to something such as a jacket or a bleacher, no penalty is assessed, and a player can restart that nugget.

● If a nugget is stuck in or behind something on purpose-to gain a time advantage for example—a penalty is assessed in the form of a berserk.

Variation: Instead of using tennis balls, use inflated balloons and play by the same rules. On "go," all the balloons are simultaneously hit upward. The team's task is to keep all the balloons from hitting the floor. If a balloon hits the floor, a berserk is applied.

Using balloons doesn't result in quite as physical a game as using tennis balls, but your players will be surprised at the physical output necessary to keep such a light item airborne.

game tip

You may have noticed that bizarre words are associated with this game. Use the new game vocabulary with confidence. New game, new rules, new vocabulary = excitement.

*L*earning Opti*o*n: *Frantic Focus*

Themes: God's peace, stress, struggles

After a few frenzies, take time out to discuss these questions:

● **How did you feel as you were playing this game?**

● **Do you ever feel that way in "real life"? If so, when?**

● **How many things can you juggle in life before your frantic, pseudo-balanced lifestyle begins to crumble?**

Calm everyone's frenzied nerves by reading aloud this verse: "You will keep in perfect peace him whose mind is steadfast, because he trusts in you" (Isaiah 26:3). Ask:

● **In our frantic lifestyles, what do people do to keep calm?**

● **What is God's promise in this verse?**

● **How can we trust God and stay focused on him in the midst of our hectic, frenzied schedules?**

Close in prayer, asking God to help students balance their frantic lives and focus on what's important—God.

Never, Never Miss

Activity Level: low

Activity Area: classroom

Supplies: players' shoes

The Game: Ask the players to sit in a circle and remove one shoe each. As kids each hold a shoe, teach them the following rhyme: "I pass this shoe from me to you; I pass like this and never, never miss."

Now teach the players to verbally accentuate every other word in the rhyme as they pick up and pass shoes. (Players pass the shoes by setting them on the floor in front of the next person.) For example:

I pass

(Pick up a shoe on "I," pass it to your right on "pass" as you accentuate the word "pass.")

this shoe

(Pick up another shoe in front of you on "this," pass it to your right on "shoe" as you accentuate the word "shoe.")

from me

(Pick up another shoe on "from," pass it to your right on "me" as you accentuate the word "me.")

to you;

(Same actions as before.)

I pass

(Same actions as before.)

like this

(Same actions as before.)

and never, never miss.

(Pick up a shoe on "and," then hold onto that shoe and pound the floor back and forth in the same rhythm—to the right, left, right—on the words "never, never miss." Let go of the shoe on "miss.")

Continue with the rhyme and more shoes, never skipping a beat. The object is to see if the group can pass the shoes around the circle without making a mistake. The first part of the rhyme is fairly easy to follow, but the "never, never miss" bit is just confusing enough to cause a shoe or two or three to jam up in one position. When that happens, the whole routine begins to break down amid much laughter and finger pointing.

Never, Never Miss is a simple and effective way to have fun for no reason.

Learning Option:
I Knew You Could Do It

Themes: affirmation, confidence, God's power, God's will

Play the game until the group experiences a certain degree of competence. Have kids congratulate one another and say, "I knew you could do it." Then say: **Sometimes when we set goals for ourselves, we wonder if we can actually achieve them. But God has promised that he will help us reach those goals if they fit within his will for our lives. If we commit those goals to God in prayer, he'll always answer.**

Have players form pairs, and have each person name a goal for the upcoming week. After they share goals, have partners tell each other, "I know you can do it."

Read 1 John 5:14-15: "This is the confidence we have in approaching God: that if we ask anything according to his will, he hears us. And if we know that he hears us—whatever we ask—we know that we have what we asked of him."

Commit the goals to God in prayer.

Pail o' Ping-Pong Balls

Activity Level: low

Activity Area: anywhere

Supplies: a gallon-sized plastic pail (with no handle) and enough Ping-Pong balls to fill the pail

The Game: Do you have a gallon-sized pail and access to a heap of Ping-Pong balls? I'm subtly suggesting that you need these supplies; otherwise we're just writing and reading. If you don't have enough Ping-Pong balls to fill the pail, put some Styrofoam "peanuts" in the bottom to take up some room. (That's not cheating, and I certainly won't tell.)

Place the pail full of Ping-Pong balls on the floor, and have the players gather around it. Say: **To be qualified, certified, and amplified, you must rotate this bucket 360 degrees through the air without spilling any Ping-Pong balls. During this complete rotation, you may not touch the Ping-Pong balls with your hands or arms. This 360-degree "circumsomething" must be purely rotational from top to bottom and back up** (see illustration)**, not a sneaky circle**

with the top oriented up for the entire rotation. The pail must be turned upside down during the rotation.

That's it. That's the entire challenge. If any Ping-Pong balls fall out of the pail, the attempt doesn't count, and you must try again after the balls have been replaced in the bucket. Be sure to encourage kids to take turns. No pail-hogging allowed!

game tip

You may want to have kids form groups and come up with possible solutions to this challenge. Then groups can vote for the best solution (without voting for their own) and work together to try that solution.

Have kids work together and pool their wisdom to come up with a solution. For example, they might come up with ideas like these:

● Use clothing to secure the Ping-Pong balls in the bucket.

● Use clear plastic wrap or aluminum foil to cover the top.

● Blindfold the facilitator so he or she can't see what the kids do.

Who knows what the solution might be?

Learning Option: Wisdom Reports

Themes: teamwork, wisdom, working together

Say: **In this game, we combined our wisdom and worked together to come up with a solution to a problem. Let's see what the Bible says about true wisdom.**

Have kids form four groups, and assign each group two of these passages:

● Psalm 51:6   ● Isaiah 33:5-6

● Psalm 111:10   ● 1 Corinthians 1:19-20

● Proverbs 4:1-7   ● Colossians 2:2-3

● Proverbs 28:26   ● James 1:5

Ask the groups to read their assigned Scripture passages and answer these questions:

● **What does each passage say about wisdom?**

● **How does it apply to life today and the problems you face?**

Have the groups share with each other what they learned.

Play Pail o' Ping-Pong Balls again, and have kids think of at least two more ways to rotate the pail of Ping-Pong balls without touching the balls with their hands or arms.

Shipwreck

Activity Level: high

Activity Area: gymnasium

Supplies: four markers such as cones, coats, or beanbags

The Game: This a classic action/reaction game the success of which depends on your enthusiasm and what you say.

Use four markers, such as cones, coats, or beanbags, to outline a large, square area (or use half a basketball court). Put up to about twenty-five players into this square. Assign each side of the square as follows: front = bow; rear = stern; left = port; right = starboard. (These designations are all relative to where you are standing and where you want the front to be.)

Since you're the captain of the vessel, the members of your crew must immediately do as they are told or
- they'll be thrown overboard to the sharks,
- they'll be forced to walk the plank, or
- they'll have to eat the captain's cooking.

(Actually, there are no penalties—just say these things to set the tone for the game.)

Here's what the crew members must do as quickly as possible and in response to your precise, well-delivered commands.
- "jellyfish"—lie on your back, with arms and legs jiggling in the air
- "sunbathing"—lie on your side
- "fish for dinner"—jump up and down, holding your nose
- "May I go to the bathroom, captain?"—salute while jumping up and down with legs crossed
- "dig for treasure"—pantomime digging movements (Sound effects are encouraged.)
- "scrub the deck"—get on hands and knees, of course
- "midships"—lie belly-down in the middle of the ship (This is funny when followed by "jellyfish" and "sunbathing.")
- "crow's-nest"—kneel on one knee and pantomime looking through a spyglass
- "bow"—run to the bow of the boat (same for stern, starboard, and port)
- "bow on fire"—run to the opposite side of the boat (same for stern, starboard, and port)

The following commands are to be done with partners:

● "overboard"—get in piggyback position

● "arm the torpedoes"—get in wheelbarrow position

● "under attack"—both partners lie on the floor with one person lying across (perpendicular) the other person's back

● "time for grub"—one person represents a table (on all fours), and the second person sits gently on his or her partner's back while "eating"

● "three in a lifeboat"—form a trio, sit on the floor single file (as on a toboggan), and row together while singing "Row, Row, Row Your Boat"

● "shipwreck"—everyone freezes

As captain of the ship, deliver the commands with a tongue-in-cheek, militaristic flair. After kids have practiced the moves, issue four or five commands in a row to provide a challenge.

Play competitively by having the last person to obey a command go out. Play noncompetitively (no elimination) just for fun.

*L*earning Opti*o*n: One Stormy Night

Themes: God's power, Jesus' life, miracles

Have all the sailors assume the "jellyfish" or "fish for dinner" position while you begin reading the story about Jesus calming the storm (Luke 8:22-25). After you read verse 24b, "He got up and rebuked the wind and the raging waters," yell, "Stop!" Have kids freeze. Then finish reading the passage.

Use this game to set the stage for other water/boat stories in the Bible. You may want to change some of the actions to reflect the specific stories:

● Noah (Genesis 6–8)—After you read Genesis 7:9, yell, "Floating zoo!" and have kids imitate their favorite animals.

● Jonah (Jonah 1–3)—After you read Jonah 1:17, yell, "Whale watching!" and have kids put their hands above their eyes and look off into the distance.

● disciples being called from their fishing boats (Matthew 4:18-22)—After you read Matthew 4:18, yell, "Gone fishin'!" and have kids pretend to cast fishing lines.

● Paul's shipwreck (Acts 27)—after you read Acts 27:44, yell, "Save yourselves!" and have kids clear the playing area.

Shooter

Activity Level: medium

Activity Area: gymnasium

Supplies: rubber bands, masking tape, three empty coffee cans, and a stopwatch

The Game: Find a place that sells large quantities of rubber bands for not much money. I recently purchased large bags of rubber bands at flea markets, more than I thought I'd ever use. So for a buck I was swimming in rubber bands, so to speak—until Shooter came along.

Use masking tape to make a line on the gym floor. Pour a copious amount of rubber bands on the floor behind the taped line. (Isn't *copious* a fine word? If you have a copious amount of something, you just don't need any more.) Place three empty coffee cans on the floor beyond the tape, open side up. The first can should sit about six feet from the tape; the next, eight feet; and the final can, twelve feet (see illustration).

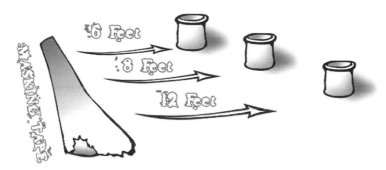

Divide the group in half. Everyone who was born in January through June should stand behind the line, and everyone who was born in July through December should spread out around the coffee cans. (Dividing a group by birthday months works almost every time.) The players behind the taped line are designated shooters, and the other half are rubber band retrievers. Everyone is on the same team. The object of the game is to score as high a point total as possible in two minutes. Rubber bands landing in the nearest coffee can earn one point apiece; those landing in the middle coffee can earn three points apiece;

and the ones that land in the farthest coffee can earn seven points apiece.

Here are some more rules:

- A rubber band must be shot, not thrown.
- The retrievers can pick up any errant bands and send them back to the shooters, but they must be shot back, not thrown.
- Retrievers cannot position their bodies as backboards in order to rebound long shots into the cans.
- After two minutes, retrieve the bands in the cans and tally the points to determine a total score. Include as part of the total the rubber bands that remain draped over the edges of the cans.
- Encourage the group to talk over this first attempt, then have players switch roles and try to better their score.
- After a second attempt, encourage the team to try one more time. For this final go at a "world record," let the team make all the decisions, such as how players should position themselves on the floor, who should be the shooters, and who should be the retrievers.

Variation: Instead of playing with rubber bands and coffee cans, play with plastic hoops and portable volleyball standards. Use the same rules. Attempting to throw hoops over an upright is a uniquely pleasing challenge. You'll have no trouble talking your players into giving this hoop-toss a try.

To increase the challenge for the retrievers, require that they put reverse spin on the hoops as they spin-lob them back to the throwers. If the throwers aren't alert, the hoops will roll back across the throwing line before they have a chance to grab them.

*L*earning Opti*o*n: Ready! Aim! Fire!

Themes: body of Christ, goals, God's will

Afterward, gather players for a discussion. Ask:

● **What cans received the most action?**

● **How did your team choose which can to target at any given time?**

● **Was there a technique to being an efficient retriever? shooter?**

● **Beyond aiming for the targets in this game, what do you aim for in life? What are your goals for the next year? five years?**

Have volunteers read aloud these passages about "aiming" and goals:

● 1 Corinthians 9:24-26
● 2 Corinthians 5:6-10
● 1 Timothy 6:11-16
● 2 Timothy 3:10-17

Ask:

● **According to these verses, what should we aim for in life?**

● **How can we work together to help each other aim in the right direction and reach our goals?**

Have kids form a circle and join hands. Pray aloud, asking God to direct your students' lives and to help them aim for God's will.

Play another round or two of Shooter. Afterward, give each player a rubber band as a reminder to aim for God's will. Be sure to warn students not to shoot their rubber bands at people.

Squash Ball Travel

Activity Level: high

Activity Area: gymnasium

Supplies: one six-foot-long dowel (at least an inch in diameter) and eight used tennis balls for each player

The Game: Got a bunch of old tennis balls lying around? Good, you'll need 'em for this game. If not, try gleaning them from outside a fenced tennis court.

Give each player eight tennis balls and one six-foot-long dowel. It's a functional bonus to place a commercial rubber tip on the end of each dowel—you know, like the tip on the bottom end of a pair of crutches. In fact, a crutch can be substituted nicely for a dowel in this game. With all the crutches people store in attics, maybe that's the way to go. Good idea—I'm glad we thought of it.

Gather all the players at one end of the gymnasium. Say: **The object of this game is to get from this side of the gym to the other, using only the props I have given you. You cannot make body contact with the floor. If you do, you must return to the start and try again. Ready? Go.**

The obvious—and I think only—solution is to step on the fuzzy spheres, lean on the dowel for support, and use the tennis balls as steppingstones to reach the opposite side of the gym.

There will be many turf-touches and returns to the start before most players get the feel for balancing on the tennis balls. This is definitely a trial-and-error activity, and the more error that is gladly accepted, the better.

game tip

If you have a large group and don't have enough tennis balls for everyone, simply have players take turns using the materials to cross the room.

Variation 1: Try a group challenge in which all players help one another to reach the opposite side. In this case, don't assign tennis balls; instead, just dump a bunch of them on the floor, and let the players use as many as they deem necessary to experience a satisfactory crossing. Don't give a dowel to each player; supply a few dowels for the whole group. Encourage players to make physical contact with one another to help them balance on the tennis balls.

How many dowels can the whole group use? Allow them to use whatever number you think will provide a satisfying challenge.

game tip

To ensure the safety of your players, you may want to direct everyone to wear safety gear such as elbow pads, knee pads, and wrist guards. Or you may want to use floor mats for this game.

Variation 2: Try "rafting" across the gym. You'll need more tennis balls for this variation—a lot more. Cut 3/4-inch plywood into four-by-eight-foot "rafts." Provide one raft for every group of four or five players.

Have each group of players set its plywood raft on a collection of tennis balls, pile on the plywood raft, and use rubber-tipped dowel "oars" to paddle across the gymnasium. They'll probably have to keep "feeding" the tennis balls back underneath the front of the raft to keep it moving. More than six people on a four-by-eight-foot raft will cause the tennis balls to flatten out and the raft to "sink," but that's just another part of the experiential package.

game tip

Avoid splinters by sanding the edges of whatever plywood rafts you create. Do the rafts need to be painted? No, but it sure looks nifty.

You could offer plywood rafts of various sizes, *beaucoup* balls, and a few dowel paddles, and see what happens. Whatever actually occurs, one thing is sure: The participants will have fun and more than a few laughs. And that's what's really important in this game.

Learning Option: Traveling On

Themes: Bible, faith, God's voice

After a few trips across the gymnasium utilizing this unique mode of transportation, gather the players for a study on Bible characters who made unique trips.

Choose from the following Bible characters. (The number of characters you study will depend on how many variations of the game you play.) As a group, read about the Bible traveler's life, the unique journey, and interesting things that happened along the way.

● Abram (Genesis 12–25; Hebrews 11:8-12)—He followed God without a map. God led Abram (later Abraham), through faith, to his destination.

● Moses (Exodus 13:17–16:35)—He followed a hot route to the promised land.

● Jonah (Jonah 1–2)—This traveler ran away from God (the ultimate travel guide), hopped a ship, and was swallowed by a great fish—more exciting than a cruise to a resort island.

● Jesus' disciples (Luke 10:1-24)—Jesus told them to pack lightly for their trip.

● Paul (Acts 27:1–28:16)—Although Paul's ship wrecked, he survived and continued to tell others about Jesus.

After your study, you may want to round up the participants and travel to a fast-food restaurant for a post-gathering snack.

Just for Fun

Beach Ball Bonanza

Activity Level: high

Activity Area: gymnasium

Supplies: inflated beach balls and plastic hoops

The Game: If I bring out a beach ball for a game, people rarely connect it to any particular sport, and they certainly don't remember negative sports encounters, such as being crunched by a bigger player or sitting out on the sideline. Bring out beach balls, and thoughts turn to beach, fun, and play. Try these ways to play with beach balls.

Variation 1: Thirty-Seven

Inflate one beach ball for the ensuing action. I call this game Thirty-Seven to remind myself how many times I want the players to hit the ball. Indeed, the crux of the game is to hit the ball thirty-seven consecutive times before the ball makes contact with the ground. Everyone is on the same team, so everyone is pursuing the same goal. Here are a few rules:

● Players can hit the ball with any part of their bodies.

● If a player purposely makes ball contact with his or her foot, two hits are awarded.

● If the ball makes contact with the ground before thirty-seven hits are accumulated, all points are lost.

● If a player hits the ball twice in succession, all points are lost.

● Two players can't hit the ball back and forth between themselves. If they do, all points are lost.

● It's OK to bounce the ball off the walls or ceiling.

● If the group achieves thirty-seven on the first try, inflate another beach ball, and have kids try to reach thirty-seven, quickly counting hits on both beach balls. With two balls in play, delete the two-points-for-a-kick rule.

Variation 2: Ya'll Hit

Simplicity itself. The only way to score a point is for everyone to hit the ball before the ball makes contact with the ground.

Variation 3: *Beaucoup* Balls

Inflate one beach ball for every five players. It helps if the beach balls are different colors. Follow the basic rules for Thirty-Seven. Each player who starts a particular ball must keep an accurate hit count for that ball (honor system). When a beach ball finally makes contact with the ground, the counter mentally records the number of hits and leaves the ball on the ground. Team play continues until all the beach balls have made contact with the ground. Each counter reveals his or her points for a grand group-score. Play again, trying to increase the group score.

Variation 4: Beach Ball Space Warp

You'll need one beach ball and two plastic hoops for this variation. Players hold the hoops any way they choose. The object is to score as many points as possible, following the basic rules for Thirty-Seven, plus these:

● Award one point for each strike of the ball. Award two points if the ball goes through a plastic hoop after the strike.

● The ball can go through the hoop in only one direction. It can't be hit back and forth.

● After a point is scored through a plastic hoop, that hoop must be given to another player before another point can be made through the same hoop.

● Hoops can't touch one another.

Learning Option:
Through the Hoop

Themes: forgiveness, God's love, grace, salvation

Have two people hold two plastic hoops in front of the group, as if the hoops were two targets. Distribute several inflated beach balls. Give everyone a chance to throw the beach balls through the hoops. Ask:

● **How did you feel when you got the ball through the hoop? missed the hoop?**

● **How is this like always trying to do the right thing? How is it different?**

● **How do you feel when you make mistakes? How do you feel when you've "been good"?**

● **Do you ever feel that God will love you less or give up on you if you make mistakes?**

Have everyone take another turn throwing the beach balls through the hoops. Each time kids throw, have them share one way people try to earn God's grace by "being good." For example, they might say, "Always go to church," "Always read the Bible," or "Be kind and loving to everyone." Ask:

● **Is it possible to earn God's grace? Explain.**

● **Why do you think people try to earn God's grace?**

● **Why do we think it's so important to God that we always do the right thing? Explain.**

● **What does doing the right thing have to do with God's grace?**

● **What is God's grace, and why is it so important to us?**

Ask someone to read aloud Ephesians 2:8-9: "For it is by grace you have been saved, through faith—and this not from yourselves, it is the gift of God—not by works, so that no one can boast."

Close in prayer, thanking God that we don't have to "jump through hoops" to try to earn God's grace, love, and forgiveness.

Bombouncement

Activity Level: high

Activity Area: gymnasium

Supplies: red playground balls

The Game: The anti-game Bombardment has resulted in a love-hate relationship within society in general. Some kids love it; some kids hate it, depending on skill level and the designated target. No matter how you look at it, trying to bash someone with a red playground ball in order to remove him or her from a game lacks compassion and any measurable curriculum value.

You can alter a few rules and use kids' enthusiasm for action in a different game called Bombouncement.

Have kids form two groups, and direct the groups to opposing sides of a gymnasium. Designate a center line. Players on one side of the line will try to eliminate players on the other side by bouncing the ball near an opposing player. That target *must* try to catch the ball after it has bounced. If the ball is caught, the game continues without penalty or award. If the ball is missed, the fumbling player joins the opposite team. If a player has a ball bounced nearby but far enough away that even an honest effort can't produce contact, the throw is void. If players fail to try to catch a ball bounced within their grasp, they join the other side.

These rules should allow you and other players to change Bombardment in such a way that the "I'm-gonna-getcha" fun remains, but the painful ball strikes are eliminated.

Learning Option: Bombarded

Themes: challenges, God's power, obstacles, sin, strength

Gather the players, and ask them to help you brainstorm the kinds of challenges that bombard kids. As they call out ideas, create a list on newsprint. For example, they might mention drugs, sex, war, murder, robbery, dishonesty, cheating, loneliness, and divorce.

Play another game of Bombouncement, and have kids yell words from the list as they throw. Play as before, having kids try to catch the balls. Afterward, gather kids and ask:

● **What was it like playing the game this way?**

● **How is that like the way we feel bombarded in every-day life with the things on our list? How is it different?**

● **What happened in the game when someone wasn't ready and on guard?**

● **How can we find strength to be on guard in the day-to-day bombardment we face?**

Have someone read aloud John 15:18-19: "If the world hates you, keep in mind that it hated me first. If you belonged to the world, it would love you as its own. As it is, you do not belong to the world, but I have chosen you out of the world. That is why the world hates you."

Have someone else read aloud John 16:33: "I have told you these things, so that in me you may have peace. In this world you will have trouble. But take heart! I have overcome the world."

Gather all the Bombouncement balls, and have everyone gather around them in a circle. Offer a prayer of thanks for God's strength and protection in resisting the challenges of the world.

Bump in the Dark

Activity Level: medium

Activity Area: large classroom or gymnasium

Supplies: none

The Game: Is there something therapeutic about screaming? I don't know, and I don't really wanna know; it's just fun,
and I'll leave it at that. But here's a game that involves more
screaming than you've attempted in a long time. Maybe ever.

Before the game begins, demonstrate a flat-out, lung-ripping
scream for the group. If you think it's necessary, make up a reason for doing it. You know, something like being lost and trying
to locate your group, or competing with your echo.

Then ask some volunteers to SOC it to you—that's "scream
on command." This is a challenge-by-choice game, so kids don't
have to perform if they don't want to. I'm betting you'll find that
a lot of players not only are ready to scream but will be disap-
pointed if they don't get the chance.

If you need a little more screaming practice, have kids form
two groups, and have them stand on opposing sides of the room.
Announce that you're going to have a "yell-off"—one group yells
in unison, then the other group yells back. The group that yells
more loudly gets to do it again. Then have everyone scream together. Share the scream.

OK, that's enough preliminary screaming. It's time to get serious about game yelling. The game Bump in the Dark—did you
forget we're warming up to a game?—requires screaming. Here's
why:

Appoint an "Ultimate It," but do it in such a way that no one
knows who you've appointed. Have players each close their eyes
and place one hand in the middle of a people cluster, with their
thumbs extended up. You (with your eyes closed, too) will feel
around those thumbs, choose one, and squeeze it once. The person whose thumb you've just squeezed then feels around and
squeezes another thumb twice. The twice-squozen thumb belongs to the "Ultimate It." Have players open their eyes while
you explain the rules.

Say: **In a moment, you'll close your eyes and mill around**

94

the room with your arms partially extended, palms forward. When two people make palm contact, there's a moment of hesitation. Wait to find out if one of the two is the "Ultimate It." If the "Ultimate It" is one of the two, the "Ultimate It" lets loose a full-blown scream. This scream symbolizes a metamorphosis for the silent partner, and the two players separate, knowing they're now both "It." Both of these players can now apply the scream, which continues to function as a change mechanism, changing a normal player into an "It." If two "Its" come in contact and scream together, both are neutralized and return to normal-player mentality. The only person who can't be normalized is the "Ultimate It." Close your eyes and mill.

Play for several minutes, then stop and count the number of normal players and "Its" to see which team will control the earth. Obviously, the winners are those who had the most fun.

Learning Option: Shout for Joy

Themes: joy, praise

Have the players form a circle. Let them rest their voices while you read aloud these verses from Psalms about shouting to God with joy: Psalms 20:5; 47:1-2; 65:13; 81:1-2.

Have kids name things they want to praise God for, things that make them want to shout with joy.

Then have kids form four groups, and assign each group one of the four verses. Close by having each group, one at a time, joyfully shout the verse as loudly as possible.

Cranial Catch

Activity Level: high

Activity Area: large classroom, gymnasium, or outside

Supplies: pantyhose, tennis balls, and scissors

The Game: For each player, cut the legs off a pair of pantyhose. Drop a tennis ball into each leg, and let it slip all the way down to the end. Grab the other end with both hands and slip it over your head. The ball at the end of the sock should be dangling somewhere between your sternum and bellybutton. Give each player one of these tennis-ball-in-the-pantyhose contraptions, and instruct kids to put the contraptions over their heads. Have each player randomly choose an opponent. Have opponents face each other and start twirling their tennis balls in opposite directions. The twirling motion is accomplished mostly with a distinct neck rotation, but good twirlers use their whole body; it's an impressive sight.

Opponents approach each other with tennis balls a-twirlin' and, in a final rotational thrust, cause the two spinning socks to intertwine, wrapping tightly around each other. As soon as this happens, the two players pull away from each other in at attempt to snatch the hose off the head of the opponent. Whoever succeeds is the winner and gets to go after another player.

Learning Option: Cranial Wisdom

Theme: wisdom

Invite the players to sit in a circle and give their craniums a rest. Have them use their heads to think about the following verses about wisdom.

Have volunteers read aloud Proverbs 2:6, 10; 3:13-14; 4:7; and 17:24.

Discuss what these verses say about wisdom and how their message applies to daily life. Then have each person share one insightful bit of wisdom a family member, friend, church member, or relative has shared with him or her.

Close in prayer, asking God for wisdom in our daily lives.

---

game tip

For a tip on an easy, cheap way to obtain pantyhose for this game, see Toupee Grab (p. 107).

Eggs and Chickens

Activity Level: medium

Activity Area: large classroom, gymnasium, or outside

Supplies: none

The Game: Does anyone *not* remember the game Rock-Paper-Scissors (R-P-S)? Loads of history and nostalgia are associated with this hand-to-hand, one-two-three-shoot confrontation.

A quick review of R-P-S for those who've forgotten or who need a refresher: Have players form pairs, and have partners stand or sit facing each other. Each partner decides to show one of three hand signals: rock (make a fist), paper (show a flat hand), or scissors (make a V sign with the index and middle fingers). Each partner holds a loose fist in front of the body, then says, "One, two, three, shoot!" As the numbers one, two, and three are said, partners rock their fists from side to side, and on the word "shoot," partners show their hand signals. If one player shows a rock and the other shows scissors, the rock player wins because rocks break scissors. Scissors beat paper because scissors cut paper, and paper beats rock because paper covers rocks. If players display the same hand signals, they tie.

Hurrah! Enough of the review. We're now ready for Eggs and Chickens. First have kids get into a mind-set that says unequivocally, "I am an egg!" Have them hunker down, round their shoulders, and tuck in their heads. Have each person move as an egg would move if it could, rolling around until encountering another egg. After identifying each other's scrambled or hard-boiled existence, the two players should play a quick round of R-P-S (no best two-out-of-three; this is just a one-shot deal, unless players tie). The winner becomes a chicken, and the other remains an egg.

Chickens get to stand up and, using their elbows as wings, announce to the world (via whatever "buc buc buc" translation seems appropriate or intimidating) that they're ready to take on any other chickens in R-P-S confrontations. The vanquished eggs roll around, looking for other eggs to R-P-S with in an attempt to move up the fowl ladder of success. (Eggs match with other eggs, and chickens match with other chickens.)

The winners of the chicken-vs.-chicken matches move up to the next level, "veloci-raptor," and overstate their new persona by gnashing their ferocious teeth and presenting their clawlike front feet (hands) at about chest height. The losers revert to the egg state, rolling around on the floor, looking for other eggs. (When two veloci-raptors meet, the winner remains a veloci-raptor, and the other reverts to an egg.) Personally, I kind of like the egg roll/role—not much to do, no real responsibility, and close to the ground (not so far to fall).

Keep rolling.

Learning Option: Rollin' and Growin' Along

Themes: maturity, spiritual growth

Say: **We've just seen some amazing transformations—from eggs to chickens to ferocious veloci-raptors. Let's imagine for a moment that these three roles represent certain stages of our spiritual development.** Ask:

● **How would Christians in the egg stage of spiritual development behave? in the chicken stage? in the veloci-raptor stage?**

After this discussion, have kids form three groups, and assign each group one of these roles: egg, chicken, and veloci-raptor. Each group's job is to role play characteristics it thinks Christians in that stage of spiritual development would display, from new, baby Christians all the way to great, mature Christians. (Or should I say veloci-raptors?)

Hebrews 5:12-14 is a great passage to read to wrap up the role-plays. Then close in prayer, asking for help in learning and growing closer to God throughout our lives.

Fire in the Hole

Activity Level: medium

Activity Area: large classroom or gymnasium

Supplies: inflated balloons

The Game: After finishing balloon games, such as balloon volleyball or basketball, what do you do with the inflated game equipment? Well, sure, of course you're going to break it. But don't just break the balloons. Try the following creative boomer scenario:

The first balloon-elimination plan involves two people putting an inflated balloon between them (in the vicinity of their belly-buttons) and hugging each other. Or they can do this back-to-back instead.

Have everyone get a partner and an inflated balloon. Tell this story, adding your own details as you go: **Once there were two old-timers who were trying to blow up a hill. But they didn't realize that they were using too much dynamite. In that silent, pre-explosion moment, right before the brilliant pyrotechnic display, you could hear them shout, "Fire in the hole!"**

When kids hear "Fire in the hole," they are to grab their partners, give a mighty pull, and enjoy the ballistic results. Tell the participants to go for it—there are lots of balloons left!

Variation 1: Have everyone line up in a circle and turn to the left so they're facing each other's backs. Have players place inflated balloons between their bodies again, creating an alternating balloon-person-balloon-person circle. Have everyone yell, "Fire in the hole" and simultaneously pull at each other to initiate the explosion.

Variation 2: Set up the group as in Variation 1, but encourage kids to move en masse from one end of the room to another without bursting or losing contact with a balloon. Only body pressure is allowed—no hands. If a balloon is inadvertently burst, have another

---

game tip

Use this activity after the kids in the group have gotten to know one another. Players need to have established considerable trust for person-to-person balloon-bursting to succeed.

balloon ready to take its place so the journey can continue. When the goal is reached, the players' reward for being so careful is "Fire in the hole!"

Learning Option: Trial by Fire

Themes: challenges, faith, God's power, obstacles, strength, suffering, trials

Have players sit in a circle, and give everyone a balloon.

Read 1 Peter 1:6-7: "In this you greatly rejoice, though now for a little while you may have had to suffer grief in all kinds of trials. These have come so that your faith—of greater worth than gold, which perishes even though refined by fire—may be proved genuine and may result in praise, glory and honor when Jesus Christ is revealed." Ask:

● **What kinds of trials do you face?**

● **How do trials "refine" our faith?**

● **How difficult is it for you to "greatly rejoice" even though you face tough times?**

● **Under what difficult circumstances has your faith become more genuine? How?**

Have kids join hands for prayer. Ask God to help us be strong when we face tough times. Offer thanks for the way tough times can help faith to grow stronger.

Have kids stand in a circle, facing clockwise, and place the balloons between them. On the count of three, have them squeeze into each other to burst the balloons and shout, "Amen!"

Tails! You're It!

Activity Level: high

Activity Area: large classroom, gymnasium, or outside

Supplies: a coin

The Game: Gather the players in one area. Have a player flip a coin into the air (doesn't matter who, just someone who has a coin), and have every player declare a heads-or-tails affiliation by placing one hand either on his or her head or on his or her behind. If the coin comes up heads, heads are "It." All the heads then charge about, trying to tag all the tails (but not *on* their tails, of course).

Have all the players maintain their hand positions while running. Then, if a tail is tagged, he or she indicates a tagged status by putting *both* hands on his or her posterior and standing with legs well spread. Uncaught tails can free tagged tails by crawling through the tagged players' legs and yelling, "Tails free!"

If a coin comes up tails, tails are "It." When a head is tagged, he or she puts both hands on top of his or her head and freezes with legs spread apart. Uncaught heads can free their frozen teammates by crawling through their legs and yelling, "Heads free!"

Shorten this game by instructing tagged players to kneel on one knee, indicating that they're out. The game continues until only a few uncaught players remain.

Variation 1: If the coin comes up heads, tails are "It," and if the coin comes up tails, heads are "It"—just a little facilitator chicanery.

Variation 2: Instruct the players to switch roles every time they're tagged, instead of freezing (switching their hand positions to display a change of affiliation).

Learning Option: In God We Trust

Themes: God's power, trust

Have kids form a circle and sit down. Look at the coin you flipped and read aloud, "In God we trust." Or point out to students the image that appears on the coin, and encourage them to discuss why that particular image was chosen to appear on the coin.

Read Psalm 146:3-4: "Do not put your trust in princes, in mortal men, who cannot save. When their spirit departs, they return to the ground; on that very day their plans come to nothing." Ask:

● **Who are some people, like the "princes and mortal men" that the psalmist described, who we tend to trust in today?**

● **Why does the Bible warn us against trusting in people?**

● **Why does God want us to trust him?**

Pass the coin around the circle, and have each person name one way he or she wants to trust in God, rather than in people, over the upcoming week.

When the coin returns to you, flip it and play one more game of Tails! You're It!

T_O*tally Tag*

Activity Level: high

Activity Area: large classroom, gymnasium, or outside

Supplies: none

The Game: I used to like Tag games because I was a decent runner. I knew kids who dreaded Tag because they knew they would be "It" forever. I'm not writing this as a nostalgic reminder of happy running times, but rather to assuage those "It" fears and to let you know that the following Tag games can be fun for everyone.

Variation 1: Todo el Mundo Tag

Everyone is "It." That's pretty much all there is to this variation. There are a few rules, however:

● Have everyone spread out before you start the game. Don't start the game with the word "go"; instead, use another word. There are a zillion other words that would work, such as "cheetah" or "zucchini." Try a bizarre one.

● If someone tags another person, the tagged person is out. The person kneels on one knee to signify his or her "out" status.

● If two people tag each other at the same time, they're both out.

● If two people tag at the same time but there's a difference of opinion as to who got who first, they're both out.

● Part of the joy of this variation is that each round ends quickly. But if you happen to have three or four die-hard competitors who don't want to confront one another, invoke the "attack" rule. All movement must be toward the opponent. Any lateral or backward moves, and you're out.

● Head tags don't count. This rule keeps fingers away from eyes.

Variation 2: Sore Spot Tag

Sore Spot Tag is an extended version of Todo el Mundo. Isn't that satisfying? You already know how to play. Just add these simple rules for a totally different Tag experience:

● Whatever part of your anatomy is touched, you must hold

that spot with one of your hands—an imaginary bandage if you will. But you're still in the game.

● If you're tagged a second time, cover that tagged spot with your other hand. And you're still in the game. (Have you figured out yet that creative tagging is one of the not-so-subtle strategies employed in Sore Spot Tag?)

● After two touches, the only tagging mechanism remaining is your hip.

● After you've been tagged a third time, you're mercifully out of the game. Kneel on one knee, and enjoy watching the remainder of the game.

Variation 3: Elbow Tag

Ask everyone to dyad-up (that is, form pairs).

Have partners stand side-by-side and link elbows. Tell them that this arm-link-with-a-partner stance signifies a temporarily "safe" position.

Next, choose one person to be "It" and another person to be the "chasee." Here are the rules:

● To be safe, the chasee must link elbows with someone. The chasee can link elbows with anyone he or she wants to. When this happens, the other person in that pair is released (triple linking isn't allowed). The released person is now the chasee. The new chasee tries to link up with someone else before "It" tags him or her.

● When "It" finally catches its prey (by tagging below the head), the caught person becomes the new "It," but he or she must spin 360 degrees before trying to tag someone. The previous "It" should run fast and link with someone before the new "It" tags him or her.

● Sometimes, when the chasee links with a pair, the now-disengaged member of that pair is quickly tagged by an alert "It." That tagged (and usually befuddled) person is not required to rotate 360 degrees before giving chase.

● All linked pairs are allowed to walk around the playing area while the chasing is going on.

● If fast runners are tediously extending the game, evoke the six-step rule. When a person breaks free of a dyad, he or she can take a maximum of six steps before he or she must relink. If someone takes more than six steps, that person is automatically and conceptually tagged.

Variation 4: Inside-Outside Tag

Have everyone line up in a circle. Have all the players count off by twos. All ones face toward the center of the circle; all twos face out. Be sure players leave some room between themselves and others.

Ask for a volunteer "It" and a volunteer chasee. The chasee begins inside the circle. "It" starts and remains outside the circle. "It" can't enter the circle. If the chasee remains inside the circle, this would be an extremely boring game if not for the following rules:

● "It" can transfer his or her "Itness" by tagging one of the players facing the circle's center (a one). That tagged player can then pursue the chasee inside the circle. If the chasee runs outside the circle, "It" must tag one of the players facing away from the circle's center (a two). That tagged player can then pursue the chasee outside the circle.

● Extolling the virtues of exercise and reasonable risk-taking, determine the number of times a chasee can weave in and out of the circle before being caught by the team.

● Once a chasee is caught, choose a new chasee, and keep playing.

Learning Option: Flee!

Themes: challenges, gossip, hate, obstacles, sin, strength, temptation, trials, worry

Play any of the Tag variations, then gather for a discussion. Ask:

● **What was it like, running away from "It" during our game?**

● **How is this like running from temptation?**

● **What tempts people in real life?**

Read James 1:12, and point out to students that it's important to persevere under trials because when we stand the test, God will give us the crown of life.

Encourage students to talk about times they have stood

strong in the face of temptation. Celebrate those times with the group, then continue the fun by playing another Tag variation.

With this variety of Tag games, you'll need a variety of topics for discussion. Try any of these "flee from" topics:

- flee from hate (Matthew 5:43-48)
- flee from worry (Matthew 6:25-34)
- flee from sin (Galatians 5:19-26)
- flee from gossip (James 3:1-12)

$T_O$upee Grab

Activity Level: high

Activity Area: gymnasium or outside

Supplies: pantyhose and tennis balls

The Game: L'eggs (correct, the company that makes pantyhose) must be extremely conscientious about its manufacturing process. How do I know that, and why do you need to know? Because pantyhose leftovers make great game supplies, and I've been buying them for next to nothing for years.

Here's the deal. For whatever reason, L'eggs gets rid of *beaucoup* pantyhose each year, making them available to nonprofit agencies for only the cost of shipping. What do you actually receive? A large cardboard box full of white (that's your only color choice) pantyhose legs—no torso connections, just legs.

I'm telling you about this because you need pantyhose legs for this game, and you shouldn't pass up such a good deal.

If the pantyhose you use don't happen to have feet in them, tie a knot in one end, then drop in a tennis ball and let it slip all the way down to the knot. Or if you're using regular pantyhose legs with feet, just drop the ball into the foot end.

Grab the other end with both hands and slip it over your head as if it were a skullcap. The ball at the end of the sock should be dangling down somewhere between your sternum and bellybutton. (This dangling distance is a safety factor—it keeps the ball away from a participant's eyes—but is not critical to how the game is played.)

game tip

If you want to go the L'eggs route, call (803) 423-4100 to order some. If not, have kids raid their homes and find pantyhose to bring in. All they need is the leg portions.

Say: **It's Toupee Grab time. You are each wearing a toupee on your head. Everybody's "It" at the outset, and each person will snatch toupees off other players' heads. The person who has the most toupees at the end of the game...has the most toupees, then everyone gets to play again.**

Here are a few more rules:

● You can't use your hands to control the hose on your head (in other words, no hands-on-own-hose).

● When your hose is snatched, sit down where you are and enjoy the action.

● If your hose is snatched then dropped, you get to retrieve it, put it on, and continue playing.

Learning Option: Greedy Grabbing

Themes: generosity, greed, materialism, money, trust, wealth

Have players bring their last batch of grabbed toupees and sit in a circle. Ask:

● **How did you feel when you were playing this game?**

● **How is snatching "toupees" off people's heads like being greedy in life? How is it different?**

● **What kinds of things do others have that you want?**

Have one person read aloud Proverbs 15:27: "A greedy man brings trouble to his family, but he who hates bribes will live." Ask:

● **What kinds of troubles does greed bring?**

Have another person read aloud Proverbs 28:25: "A greedy man stirs up dissension, but he who trusts in the Lord will prosper." Ask:

● **Why do you think greed causes dissension?**

● **How can trusting in the Lord help a person prosper?**

Have the people holding toupees "generously" give them back to people who have none. Then have kids form pairs. Have partners talk about things they are greedy for. Then have pairs close in prayer, asking God to help them trust him in all things.

Indexes

Scripture Index

Theme Index

Activity-Level Index

Activity-Area Index